NORTH FOR UNION

PRESIDENT JAMES K. POLK

From an 1846 painting by G. P. A. Healy
Copy in the Tennessee Historical Society Collections

NORTH FOR UNION

John Appleton's Journal
Of a Tour to New England
Made by President Polk
In June and July
1847

Edited By

WAYNE CUTLER

Vanderbilt University Press

Nashville, Tennessee

1986

Library of Congress Cataloging-in-Publication Data

North for Union.

    Includes bibliographical references.
    1. United States—Politics and government—War with Mexico, 1845–1848.
2. United States—History—War with Mexico, 1845–1848—Public opinion.
3. Polk, James K. (James Knox), 1795–1849—Journeys—New England.
4. Appleton, John, 1815–1864—Diaries. 5. New England—Description and
travel—1775–1865. 6. Public opinion—United States—History—19th century.
I. Cutler, Wayne, 1938–   .   II. Appleton, John, 1815–1864.
E407.N67   1986   973.6'1   86–9162
ISBN 0–8265–1217–8

For my wife,
Leta Harriet Rush Cutler
and our daughter,
Lori Catherine Cutler

Preface

Anticipating that during his forthcoming tour of the Northeast he would have neither time nor energy to keep his diary current, President James K. Polk skipped forty pages between his entries for June 22 and July 7, 1847. Clearly the President intended to make retrospective entries for the intervening fifteen days of intensive travel and speech making. With that purpose in view Polk turned to John Appleton, Chief Clerk of the Navy Department, to write a journal of the northern tour; and upon receipt of Appleton's rather lengthy account, Polk found that he had left too few pages blank. He briefly noted where he had travelled on each of the fifteen days and retained Appleton's bound manuscript as an addendum to his presidential diary.

Following the death of the President in 1849, John Appleton's Journal remained in the custody of Mrs. Polk until her death in 1891. In 1897 Mrs. Polk's niece and heir, Mrs. George W. Fall, gave Appleton's Journal to Judge Jacob McGavock Dickinson, in whose family's possession the bound manuscript remained until 1926. On October 22, 1926, Jacob McGavock Dickinson, Jr., gave the Journal to the Polk Memorial Association of Nashville to be kept with other Polk memorabilia under the Association's custodianship. Generations of historians have had but scanty knowledge of the existence of this rare and illuminating account of President Polk's war-time travels north for Union. Now for the first time John Appleton's Journal is presented in published form, some one hundred thirty-nine years after its composition.

Journal Sources. John Appleton, born in 1815 and graduated from Bowdoin College in 1834, studied law at Cambridge Law School and practiced his profession in Portland, Maine, before assuming the editorship of the *Eastern Argus* in 1838. He served as chief clerk of the Navy Department from 1845 to 1848. He was confirmed as U.S. minister to Bolivia on March 30, 1848, and saw a year's service on that mission, which ended with the close of the Polk administration. He won election to a seat in the U.S. House in 1851, following which term he resumed the practice of law. During the Buchanan administration he served as assistant secretary of the State Department, 1857-60, and as U.S. minister to Russia, 1860-61. He died in Portland on August 22, 1864.

Appleton was, of course, a firsthand witness to all of the events about which he wrote, excepting the President's return trip from Portsmouth to Washington. For local reactions, texts of speeches, and names of host dignitaries, Appleton relied on press reports, chief among which were those rather extensive accounts written by "The Doctor" for the *New York Herald*. In general the Democratic and independent newspapers gave full and sympathetic treatment to the President's tour, and the Whig journals accorded it minimal and grudging coverage. Appleton's observations from inside the President's suite provide an important albeit biased perspective, for it probably reflects the President's point of view in most instances. In any case, Polk himself wrote very little about his journey, and for want of any better evidence Appleton's account supplies the best available mirror of Polk's thinking on the subject.

Editorial Method. Always concerned that the reader's primary focus fall on the text of the Journal and Correspondence, the editor has limited his annotations to the identification of Polk's correspondents and their oblique references of consequence. For identification of persons mentioned only by surnames in the Journal, the reader will want to consult the index. The editor has rendered the text faithfully with a strict regard for original punctuation and orthography, except for the following rules of normalization: (1) initial words of sentences have been capitalized and ending punctuation marks have been supplied; (2) conventional spellings have been followed except when misspellings have been clearly written; (3) conventional upper and lower case usage has been followed when the author employed multiple and/or irregular forms of the same character, thus indicating no discernible meaning behind his usage of capitals; (4) cancellations and unintentional word repetitions have been ignored unless something more than writing errors are indicated; (5) regardless of their position in the original manuscript, the salutation, place of composition, and date appear on the line or lines immediately below the document's heading; and (6) superscripts have been brought down to the line.

The following symbols have been used in the headnotes to indicate each document's classification and repository:

AE	Autograph Endorsement
AN	Autograph Note
ALS	Autograph Letter Signed
DLC	Library of Congress
JKP	Papers of James K. Polk
L	Letter
LS	Letter Signed

Acknowledgments. It is with pleasure that the editor expresses his deep appreciation to members of the Polk Memorial Association for their strong support of this publication project. In particular he would thank Virginia W. Alexander for her excellent counsel in planning and executing this work. James P. Cooper, Jr., Cecilia S. Cornell, Leta R. Cutler, Dana H. Herbert, Ross R. Mason, and Carese M. Parker provided valuable research and staff assistance, and for their most helpful service he is greatly in their debt. Illustrations are reproduced from the collections of the Library of Congress.

Vanderbilt University   WAYNE CUTLER

Contents

Chronology

OUTBOUND

June 22   From Washington City to Baltimore by cars

June 23   From Baltimore to Wilmington by cars; from Wilmington to Philadelphia by steamer *Washington*

June 25   From Philadelphia to South Amboy by cars; from South Amboy to New York City by steamer *Vanderbilt*

June 27   From New York City to New Haven by steamer *Hero;* from New Haven to Hartford by cars; from Hartford to Springfield by cars

June 29   From Springfield to Boston by cars

July 1   From Boston to Concord by cars; from Concord to Lowell by cars

July 2   From Lowell to Portland by cars; from Portland to Hallowell by steamer *Huntress;* from Hallowell to Augusta by carriage

xiii

INBOUND

July 3   From Augusta to Gardiner by carriage; from Gardiner to Portland by steamer *Huntress*

July 5   From Portland to Portsmouth by cars; from Portsmouth to Boston by cars; from Boston to Fall River by cars; from Fall River to New York City by steamer *Bay State*

July 6   From New York City to Princeton, Trenton, and Philadelphia by cars

July 7   From Philadelphia to Baltimore and Washington City by cars

Introduction

In John Appleton's Journal scholars will find the record of an insider's view of President James K. Polk's tumultuous receptions in Baltimore, Philadelphia, New York, Boston, Concord, and Augusta.[1] Historians unfriendly to "Mr. Polk's War" generally have played down the popularity of his presidency in the northern states, leaving his place in history rather more negative than that allowed by his contemporaries. Appleton's Journal provides a partial corrective to the notion that northerners generally opposed both the Mexican War and the President under whose personal direction the conflict was expanded and fought.[2]

Appleton's Journal claims another point of uniqueness. Seldom in one historical record do national and local history blend together so completely. Local responses to Polk's tour had indirect national consequences; on the other hand, Polk's tour revealed much of what local leaders thought was consequential for the President to see and experience in their community. For example, New Yorkers thought that their local water aqueduct was truly one of the wonders of their great city. Boston's Whig leaders proudly pointed to their free public schools as "the peculiar institution" of the North. Thus the reader of the Journal "sees" the northeastern urban centers as Polk and local leaders saw the state of their civilization, including its architecture, humanitarian institutions, industrial progress, commercial growth, and perhaps most importantly, its people.

President Polk's correspondence provides a different, though

related perspective from which to examine this very important
trip northward.   Many of the letters, of course, convey official invitations and presidential responses; others detail partisan
infighting between local Democrats and Whigs with respect to
Polk's visit. Viewing the letters collectively and in tandem with
Appleton's Journal, the reader learns firsthand the divisive effects
of the nation's war with Mexico and Polk's personal efforts to contain the growth of anti-war sentiment in the Northeast, much of
which had been nurtured and fed by opposition newspapers in the
first year of the war.

No negative aspect of the War's management in Washington
escaped the attention of the Whig press in America. Conversely,
Democratic newspapers knew no bounds in their praise of the
President's expansionist policies. It would be but a slight exag-
geration to say that an unbiased, nonpartisan press barely existed
during the second party system, and those newspapers without
specific party backing often took decided stands on the war issue,
thus slanting their news coverage as suited their owner's point of
view. The party presses devoted their columns almost entirely to
political affairs and to commercial concerns. The more independent or "sensationalist" sheets extended their coverage to those
remarkable and timely events that commanded two cents worth
of curiosity from the reader on the street. The twopenny presses
lived on the excitements of the day, not the annual subscriptions
of the party faithful. Although the popular presses may have
overdramatized their news stories, their attention almost always
certified the reality of like public tastes and interests.[3]

Appleton's Journal, Polk's correspondence, and newspapers
are not the kinds of evidence with which to quantify what may
have been the political consequences of his trip. However interesting such calculations might be, their use would probably prove
misleading, for neither the President nor his opponents expected
the electorate's political persuasions to be greatly changed by the
demonstration of presidential power or the charisma of its standard bearer. Electioneering in the second party system seldom
turned many voters away from the principles of their fathers. No,
the function of the political rally was to arouse the voting corps
to unity and action. For most voters, the decisive choice came

on the question of whether or not to vote. Viewed in that special sense of the word *political*, Polk could say quite truthfully that he planned to make a "non-political" excursion, for most of the eastern congressional elections had already been held.[4]

Like three of his southern predecessors, James Monroe, Andrew Jackson, and John Tyler, Polk traveled to New England to pay his respects to her citizens and solicit their continued regard for the Union. The symbolism of his journey might be easily misread or quickly dismissed without careful examination of the young republic's conflicting concepts of the Union. In the election of 1844 the American people had confronted for the first time in their history an explicit and unequivocal choice between expansion and consolidation. Would they think of the Union in terms of an agrarian frontier or a trading commonwealth, the mindsets for both of which had derived from the colonial past.

Over 150 years of colonial experience had proved how difficult it was for civil and military governance to break down the psychological barriers of frontier isolation and its attendant rule of local self-interest. The English plantations in North America had begun literally at the water's edge with inadequate capitalizations, inexperienced leadership, and indeterminate development strategies. American colonization had progressed not as a national program of expansion but as sundry localized efforts to achieve limited financial and sectarian goals. In the process of locating and settling the tidewater frontiers, hardship and religion had made a virtue of isolation; and self-rule thus had become all the more consequential to those having known no other choice of individual and collective identities. As colonists had moved inland and established new farms and communities, they had duplicated those patterns of local government taught by experience and had modified those practices unsuitable to new circumstances. For its part the crown had chosen to allow the colonists exceptional measures of civil and religious self-determination, largely because any alternative course would have proved too costly to sustain. On the frontier, individual thought and action had become normative both for reasons of preference as well as necessity.

Unlike the frontier colonials, who formed the bulk of the producing classes, substantial numbers of British subjects in the

American colonies had gained sufficient status, or expectation thereof, to cross over the physical, mental, and emotional barriers of their locality. These Atlantic colonials had not lived as western pioneers, but had looked eastward from their port cities and had found release from their new-world isolation. They had wanted to recreate in the new world the mores of the old; and in seeking that more cosmopolitan outlook, they had conserved an English culture more exaggerated and fixed than that of the old country. Their local center of authority and respectability had become that of the colonial governor's court, for however minor its standing in the ranks of the old aristocracy, it had provided an otherwise unavailable measure of social and economic stability. Those who feared frontier anarchy more than imperial tyranny had sought their place and protection within government's consolidating powers, despite the limitations of its provincial reach. Both the frontier and the Atlantic perspectives would survive the course of republican revolution and political division within the new republic.

Early in their development the New World's first thirteen republics had faced a common struggle to define the objectives of their revolutions and the bases of their associated war for independence. Each of the disaffected British colonies had experienced like dangers—economic, civil, and military—on the obscure edges of a global commonwealth; but each of the American outposts had linked itself more closely to the empire's center than to its nearest sister colony. No two of the settlements had shared like historical and legal relationships to crown, parliament, and proprietary interest. Ministerial efforts in the 1760's to consolidate imperial rule had met with varying measures of colonial resistance, and after a decade of uneven legislative decisions the King's ministers had yet persisted in underestimating the difficulty and costs of reversing the crown's long-standing policy of salutary neglect. In fighting their common war for political separation, leaders of the thirteen colonial revolutions had learned in great depth and with no little frustration their own limited capacities for united action.[5]

Polk was a grandson of both the revolution and the frontier, and in his view of history the Constitutional fathers had established a frontier Union, "an empire of liberty," as Thomas

Jefferson had phrased it. This republican experiment in self-government had thrust upon the minds of subjected peoples on three continents the new and revolutionary vision of limited government. By treaty thirteen sovereign states had agreed to create a general government and had assigned to it a small number of specific and exclusive powers to exercise in their behalf. The terms of this compact and its first ten amendments had promised, among other things, that the general government would not be used to create a privileged class, control the market place, or establish a state religion. Considering the number of dynastic, trade, and religious wars that had been fought to establish and maintain such important prerogatives, those with more sceptical minds in 1789 had thought that government so restrained and weakened must soon fall prey to anarchy or foreign domination. Those with more sensitive scruples had judged it a peculiar republic wherein the majority race extolled the virtues of freedom and yet accepted and protected the institution of slave labor.

Among the counsels of frontier republicans such practical and idealistic reservations had not proved persuasive; indeed, no experiment in limited union could have been launched without taking great risks and making many compromises. In the public debates over the Constitution's ratification, frontier republicans had objected that the general government's powers would be too great; and the newly-washed Atlantic republicans had argued that the plan would just barely correct the basic defects of the original Articles of Confederation. Between those two polarities of thought had developed a minimal consensus in favor of the compact and its prospective amendments. Thomas Jefferson's election to the presidency in 1801 and the subsequent embarrassment of Atlantic republicans meeting at Hartford in 1814 had seemed to enlarge the Constitutional consensus and tilt its interpretation in favor of frontier republicanism. Yet the tilting had been more of a seeming than a fundamental shifting.

Family tradition had dictated that Polk become a political disciple of Jefferson's Democratic-Republican Party.[6] Reared on the frontiers of North Carolina and Tennessee, Polk had experienced the isolation of rural life and had learned the common wisdoms of agrarian expansion. Both by necessity and choice American frontiersmen had pressed the boundaries of land cultivation as their principal margin of economic opportunity; to sons of the soil, territorial expansion had not meant the conquering of settled, productive populations, but rather the overcoming of nature's harsh and unrelenting rule of caprice and scarcity. Polk's father, Samuel, had made his fortune in the great American migration, and he had formed close and lasting friendships with Andrew Jackson and other leading land surveyors with whom he had worked the western district of Tennessee. For family business reasons Sam Polk had wanted his eldest son to have a proper education.

Young James had attended the University of North Carolina and had won first honors in Latin and mathematics, class of 1818. At Chapel Hill he also had acquired considerable distinction for his literary club debates; as president of the Dialectic Society he had led his fellow debaters into weekly argumentation of the day's current issues. On one occasion the Di's had considered whether or not further westward expansion would be expedient. Although no notes on the points of this debate have survived, the affirmative line of argument probably followed traditional tenets of the Jeffersonian dogma. Continued westward expansion would insure diffusion of both wealth and power; without this distribution of agrarian opportunity, the forces of consolidated wealth would gain control of the general government and turn its taxing powers to the greater advantage of the monied few. Once the general government had become a great power to be greatly prized, state and regional jealousies would so intensify and divide the states as to render voluntary or free union both unworkable and undesirable. Further expansion was essential to free union. After college Polk had studied law under one of Tennessee's most able lawyers and prominent Democrats, Felix Grundy of Nashville. Within seven years of his graduation from college, Polk had begun the practice of law, served in Tennessee's General Assembly, and won election to Congress. Family traditions, collegiate experiences, and professional connections had led him to choose the Jeffersonian dogma that was so popular among frontier republicans of his day.

Polk had won his first election to Congress in 1825, the

year after Henry Clay of Kentucky had proposed his consolidating plans for an American System of centralized banking, internal improvements, and protective tariffs. Polk had supported Andrew Jackson's presidential bid and without reservation had judged John Q. Adams guilty of having bargained his way into the presidency, thus corrupting the highest office of public trust in the gift of a free electorate. On what moral basis could a republic claim its fundamental authority if its lawmakers themselves debased the selection process and thus indirectly the will of the people to rule themselves justly, if at all? In his fourteen years of congressional service Polk had opposed consolidating measures of every description, first as Jackson's floor leader in the House and then as Speaker of that body. As governor (1839-41) and party leader in Tennessee, Polk had supported the North-South alliance of the Old Democracy, even though those attachments had meant loss of his gubernatorial races in 1841 and 1843.

In nominating Polk for president in 1844, the Democracy had reaffirmed its fundamental creed that America's ongoing agrarian migration westward was not just an appendage of the 1789 Constitutional consensus, but its very animus for a voluntary Union. All four of Polk's campaign pledges—to establish a republican government in Oregon, to acquire Texas and California, to set up an independent Treasury system, and to lower tariffs—had bespoken the frontier agenda of an expanding republic dedicated to the principle of limited government, an "empire of liberty" as it had become and must remain. His Whig opponent, Henry Clay, had argued that further expansion might lead the republic into war with Britain or Mexico or both and thus place in grave jeopardy the wealth, unity, and safety of the nation, the true interests of which might be better served by binding the nation together with a new central bank and continued protection for domestic manufactures and employments. Northern antislavery elements of the Whig Party had demanded the prohibition of slavery in the western territories; and had those dissidents not defected to the Liberty Party in substantial numbers, particularly so in New York State, Clay would have won the election. Polk had carried the Electoral College with 170 out of 275 votes, but by a small margin had failed to win a majority of the popular vote.

In choosing between Polk and Clay the American electorate
had split into almost equal halves over the meaning of the
republic's history and its concept of union.   Future historians
would debate the significance of the frontier's closing in the 1890's,
but it was not the lack of virgin soil that brought the second
republic to its violent end in the 1860's.   By 1844 the Union's
margin of constitutional consensus had shrunk beyond the point
of safety, with or without further expansion, free of slavery or
otherwise.   Had Clay won the presidency and blocked further
western migrations, the secession crisis of 1861 probably would
have come a decade earlier. Polk's defense of Texas and his ac-
quisition of Oregon, New Mexico, and California would mask the
deeply rooted splits in the body politic; in due course President
Lincoln would fight and win the war for consolidation that the
British had lost and the Constitutional fathers had avoided.

President Polk had formed an able though not very clever
cabinet, the membership of which was representative of the
party's many divisions.   Secretary of State James Buchanan
of Pennsylvania was a northerner with southern principles and
strong presidential ambitions.   Treasury Secretary Robert J.
Walker of Mississippi was a confirmed advocate of the sub-
treasury system with a sense of balance on the tariff question.
Secretary of War William L. Marcy of New York was an expansionist with ties to the anti-Van Buren wing of his state party.
Attorney General John Y. Mason of Virginia was a former member of John Tyler's cabinet with several years of prior experience
as a U.S. district judge. Postmaster General Cave Johnson of
Tennessee was a devoted friend of the President's with many
close connections among Van Buren's friends in Congress. Navy
Secretary George Bancroft of Massachusetts was a published his-
torian with a known bias for writing the way he voted. In matters great and small Polk had consulted his cabinet, but in most
decisions he had followed judgments largely of his own making.

In the first eighteen months of his administration the
President had accomplished the domestic side of his program.
Equipped with nominal Democratic majorities in both houses
of Congress and experienced in legislative management, Polk
had lobbied his tariff reductions and Treasury reforms through

their third readings, despite strong Whig resistance and tricky Democratic infighting. None of the old party wounds inflicted before and during the 1844 Democratic Convention had healed, for Polk had agreed on the occasion of his nomination not to serve, if elected, more than a single term. Those with lingering presidential ambitions had taken their new party leader at his word and had begun their 1848 campaigns well in advance of Polk's inaugural. Yet divisions within the Democracy had developed for reasons more substantial than personal preference. Many Northern Democrats had shifted ground on the tariff question because of increased local manufacturing and public sensitivity to cheaper foreign products. Resolute southern opposition to protection had provided fertile ground for the growth of anti-slavery sentiment in the North. Conservative or soft-money Democrats had worried that Polk's Treasury reforms would force their state banks out of business. Whig internal improvement projects had undercut popular support of the Old Democracy in state elections, and thus younger Democrats had found themselves cut off from the lower rungs of the political ladder. Domestic issues had ripped gaping holes in the fabric of Jackson's mantle; and had Polk's disputes with Britain and Mexico gone poorly, the republic's youngest president to date might have been its last.

Polk had answered in his Inaugural Address those critics, domestic and foreign, who had accused him of planning an expansionist war of aggression on his neighbors. Foreign powers had not understood the true character of the United States government:

Our Union is a confederation of independent States, whose policy is peace with each other and all the world. To enlarge its limits is to extend the dominions of peace over additional territories and increasing millions. The world has nothing to fear from military ambition in our Government. While the Chief Magistrate and the popular branch of Congress are elected for short terms by the suffrages of those millions who must in their own persons bear all the burdens and miseries of war, our Government can not be otherwise than pacific.[7]

To be certain, he had given no ground on the right of the Republic of Texas "to merge her sovereignty as a separate and independent state in ours." Nor had he backed down on the Oregon issue, for he had thought that the United States' claim to that territory was "clear and unquestionable" and that said title was now being perfected by the settlement of immigrants with wives and children in their company. The assumption of his argument had been that governmental claims to unoccupied territory were nominal until validated by the sovereignty of the land's occupants, for the Creator had made the earth for man and not otherwise. Like generations of frontier republicans before him, he had begun with the premise that man's right to rule nature included the right of self-government. He had not questioned the extent or timing of the westward migration, for in the tradition of the republic its manifest destiny had been in the hands of its plowmen, not its government. The Republic of Mexico had opened its doors to immigration without pressure from the United States government; and now that Texans had established their independence from Mexican consolidation, they had won the choice of self-determination. By treaty the United States and Great Britain had agreed to joint occupational rights in Oregon; and the tide of American settlement in that territory had carried with it the perfecting powers of occupants' rule.

Within weeks of Polk's taking office Mexico had broken diplomatic relations with the United States. On June 15, 1845, Polk had ordered Zachary Taylor to move from his base at Fort Jessup, Louisiana, to the western frontier of Texas; and by July 31 Taylor had set up camp on the south bank of the Nueces River, from which position he was to move against any Mexican force crossing the Rio Grande into Texas. From the Mexican point of view the United States had sent an army of invasion into Mexico to make good on its illegal annexation of Texas; the point of Taylor's invasion had begun not at the Nueces or the Rio Grande but at the Sabine River, Mexico's eastern border. In September Polk had dispatched John Slidell to Mexico, hoping that Mexico would resume full diplomatic relations and agree to the U.S. annexation of Texas, the sale of upper California and New Mexico, and the settlement of Mexico's debts to U.S. claimants. Mexico had not agreed to receive a U.S. minister, and in December had rejected his credentials. On the last day of the year General Mariano Paredes, who was then in the secret employ of the Spanish crown, overthrew Mexican President Jose J. Herrera. Spain had hoped that if Paredes could provoke a war crisis, the Mexican army would turn to the monarchist party for the restoration of the Bourbon throne.[8] In January Paredes had pledged to defend Mexico's territorial claims, and Polk had ordered Taylor to the Rio Grande. On May 8, 1846, Polk had learned of the outbreak of hostilities and three days later had asked Congress for a declaration of war, the sanction of which had come on May 13. In the winter and spring of his first year in office, Polk had faced difficult decisions on the Texas question and at the same time had risked the dangers of war with Great Britain over Oregon.

On December 27, 1845, Richard Pakenham, British minister to the United States, had proposed that the question of a partition of Oregon at the 49th parallel be submitted to arbitration. Polk had rejected Pakenham's overture and had sent to Congress a request for a resolution terminating joint Anglo-American occupation of Oregon. Congress had given its approval on April 27, and in less than two weeks both nations had learned of the fighting on the Rio Grande. Within a week of receiving that intelligence, the British cabinet had authorized Pakenham's direct settlement of the Oregon boundary at the 49th parallel. Whether by accident or design Polk's hard line on the Texas and Oregon disputes had demonstrated to the British government that the President was prepared to fight a two-front war. Pakenham had lost no time in arranging productive discussions, and on June 15 the U.S. Senate had given its approval to the British partition proposals. Polk had compromised his campaign pledge to fight for the whole of Oregon, but he had given up no territory then occupied by his fellow citizens. In resolving the Oregon question Polk had discharged a third campaign promise, but he had also quieted a substantial part of the expansionist fervor in the northern states.

Taylor's early victories (at Palo Alto, Resaca de la Palma, and Monterey), Robert F. Stockton's successful naval operations on the California coast, and Stephen W. Kearney's occupation of New Mexico had sustained popular support for the Mexican War through September, but by fall it had become evident that Mexico could and would make it an expensive war of no short duration. Taylor's call for an eight-week truce on September 25 had angered

his Commander-in-Chief and had handed Whig congressional can-
didates a timely argument that the President's mismanagement
of the War had left the troops in the field exposed to unneces-
sary dangers and had given supply vendors undue profits. Second
thoughts about Polk's domestic and military measures had helped
elect a narrow Whig majority in the House, although its control
would not pass to opposition hands until the meeting of the next
Congress. Buoyed by their electoral victories, Whig politicians
had heightened their level of anti-war dissent in the winter of
1847 and had demanded an end to "Mr. Polk's" unjust war for
the expansion of slavery. For his part the President had become
increasingly distrustful of his Whig generals and had sought un-
successfully to place men of his own political persuasion in command of the armies. Political extremism had gripped the counsels
of both parties, and America's winter of discontent had deepened
those divisions so clearly evident in the presidential election of
1844.

In the spring of 1847 Taylor's army had won a most difficult
battle at Buena Vista, and Winfield S. Scott's invasion force had
landed at Vera Cruz and moved inland with success at Cerro
Gordo on April 18. News of these fresh victories in Mexico had
encouraged Polk to send Nicholas P. Trist, chief clerk of the State
Department, to Mexico in search of a peace treaty. Taylor's
control of northern Mexico and Scott's movements toward Mexico
City had dispelled all hopes among Mexican elites of an outright
military victory; but given the intensity and depth of political
divisions in the United States, further delay had suggested itself
as a possible tool for Mexico's winning the peace, if not the war.
Polk had regained the political advantage at home with news of
victories at Buena Vista, Vera Cruz, and Cerro Gordo; but he
had learned from experience how little he could do on his own
initiative to deflect the criticism of his policies and to unite public
opinion, particularly in the Northeast where Whigs controlled
almost every statehouse and major city hall. Perhaps he had
stayed at his desk beyond the limits of his endurance; perhaps he
had longed to know what the American people really thought of
the War; or perhaps he had thought that a presidential progress
would show the Mexicans that his domestic opponents could not

settle on any less favorable terms than he. Polk did not put the motives for his travel plans down on paper, but he must have understood how risky it would be to visit the centers of his Whig opposition and chance the public's merely polite or even hostile response. The President went north for Union and risked the sum of his political career because the frontier consensus had to be revived and expanded. Otherwise, the states could not remain at peace with each other and thus might be lost "the only free asylum for the oppressed" left on earth.[9]

NOTES

1. A more detailed analysis of Polk's reception in the Northeast was presented as a paper and read for the 1985 Walter Prescott Webb Memorial Lecture at the University of Texas at Arlington on March 14, 1985.

2. For the most scholarly and provocative treatment of American public opinion during the Mexican War, as gleaned from the periodical literature of the period, see Robert W. Johannsen, *To The Halls of The Montezumas: The Mexican War in the American Imagination* (New York, 1985). For a specialized account of dissenting Whig opinion on the War, see John H. Schroeder, *Mr. Polk's War: American Opposition and Dissent,1846-1848* (Madison, 1973).

3. The most able of the reporters accompanying Polk was "The Doctor," who wrote for the independent *New York Herald.* Textual analysis demonstrates that Appleton borrowed heavily from "The Doctor" in detailing his account of the journey. Unfortunately Appleton did not disclose the name of his journalist friend. "The Doctor" mentioned in one of his published 1846 letters to the *Herald* that he had stayed in the Astor House in New York City on the evening of August 15, 1846; he had taken a room there again during President Polk's visit of June 25-27, 1847. George B. Wallis of Washington City registered his name at the Astor on both occasions. Wallis subsequently signed "Dr. G. B. Wallis" under his reminiscence of Lincoln's first inauguration; the publisher of that article identified Wallis as having been "A Contemporary Newspaper Correspondent at the Capital." For transcriptions of the Astor House Registers, see *New York Herald,* August 16, 1846, and June 27, 1847. For a reprint of Wallis' article on the Lincoln inauguration and his recollection of Polk's inaugural ball, see "Honest Abe and the Little Giant: A Reminiscence of Lincoln's First Inauguration," *The Outlook,* February 9, 1921. According to the *Boston Post* of July 8, 1847, "Dr Wallace, correspondent of the New York Herald, accompanied the party, as a permanent member of the unofficial suite . . . ."

4. Of the eastern seaboard states, only Maryland had not held its regular congressional elections. Some eighteen out of twenty-nine states had held congressional elections prior to June 1847; of the 161 House members chosen to date, 87 were Whigs, 71 were Democrats, and 3 were independents. The Whigs had gained 32 seats and thus expected to control the lower house; the U.S. Senate would remain solidly Democratic in the next Congress. The Democratic reverses in the early congressional elections had come, for the most part, prior to U.S. military successes in Mexico.

5. A list of the more useful books on republican ideology in the early national period might include the following works: Bernard Bailyn, *The Ideological*

Origins of the American Revolution (Cambridge, 1967) and *The Origins of American Politics* (New York, 1968); Lance Banning, *The Jeffersonian Persuasion: Evolution of a Party Ideology* (Cornell, 1978); Richard Buel, Jr., *Securing the Revolution: Ideology in American Politics, 1789-1815* (Cornell, 1972); and Gordon S. Wood, *The Creation of the American Republic, 1776-1787*. In the periodical literature see the following two works: Richard Buel, Jr., "Democracy and the American Revolution: A Frame of Reference," *William and Mary Quarterly*, XXI (1964), 165-90; and Robert E. Shalhope, "Toward a Republican Synthesis: The Emergence of an Understanding of Republicanism in American Historiography," *William and Mary Quarterly*, (1972), 49-80. For the most thorough consideration to date of the revolutionary ideology, as brought forward into the Jackson period, see Robert V. Remini, *Andrew Jackson and the Course of American Freedom, 1822-1832* (New York, 1981).

6. The most authoritative biography of Polk is a two-volume work by Charles G. Sellers, Jr., *James K. Polk: Jacksonian, 1795-1843* and *James K. Polk: Continentalist, 1843-1846* (2 vols.; Princeton, 1957 and 1966).

7. James D. Richardson, comp., *A Compilation of the Messages and Papers of The Presidents, 1789-1902* (10 vols.; Washington, D.C., 1896-1899), IV, p. 380.

8. For details of Paredes' employment by the Spanish crown and monarchist plans for a restoration government in Mexico, see Miguel Enrique Soto Estrada, "The Monarchist Conspiracy in Mexico, 1845-1846" (Ph.D. Dissertation, University of Texas at Austin, 1983).

9. Polk's Address to the Maine Legislature, July 3, 1847, in John Appleton, "Journal of a Tour to New England Made by the President in June and July 1847," Polk Memorial Association Collections, Polk Ancestral Home, Columbia, Tennessee; for the text of Polk's Address, see above, pp. 68-72.

Journal
Of a Tour to New England
Made by the President
In June and July
1847

Journal

Tuesday June 22

On the 22d. day of June A.D. 1847, the President left Washington for an excursion to the North. He contemplated visiting Baltimore, Philadelphia, New York and Boston, and hoped to be able to embrace in his journey, Concord, the Capital of New Hampshire, and Augusta, the Capital of Maine. His journey was undertaken with no political purpose, but with a desire, on his part, to observe more closely than he had ever before had opportunity to do, the institutions and the people of the northern portion of his Country, and especially to witness the condition, and to become acquainted with the inhabitants, of the States which compose New England.

The hospitalities of the principal cities on his proposed route, had been extended to him before his departure; and he had been urgently requested to visit New Hampshire and Maine, by the unanimous votes of their respective Legislatures. The most gratifying invitations had also been sent to him from other places in the North, and from a large number of Societies and individuals.

He started from the Metropolis, in a special car, by the noon train for Baltimore, and a beautiful day shone upon his departure. As far as the Monumental City, his journey was graced by the presence of his accomplished lady, who with her niece, Miss Rucker, and attended by Mr Russworm of Washington, was on her way to visit her home and friends in Tennessee. His permanent *Suite* was composed of Mr Nathan Clifford, Attorney General, Mr Edmund Burke, Commissioner of Patents, and Mr John Appleton, Chief Clerk in the Navy Department; but the party was further enlarged by the reception of Mr Frank N. McNairy and Mr Robert Weakley, two young gentlemen from the West, who embraced the opportunity afforded them by the kindness of the President, to see a portion of the Country under its most favorable aspect.

Thus accompanied, the President took leave of the White House at precisely twelve o'clock, and he was escorted to the depot by all the members of his Cabinet, by Col. Walker, his private Secretary, and a large number of other friends. Many ladies also took leave of Mrs Polk at the cars, and our journey was thus commenced under the most happy auspices.

The train had waited for us a few minutes, and dashed off, as soon as we arrived, at a rate of speed which was as exhilarating as it was unusual. Rapid, however, as was our progress, the telegraph wires which kept us company along the road, were constantly reminding us that, in comparison with the lightning line, *our* boasted conveyance was only, after all, a "slow coach," and in point of fact, the news of our departure was in Baltimore before we had reached the nearest border of Bladensburg. But magnetism carries no passengers, and we were contented, therefore, to abide the less marvellous but more serviceable results of Steam. Nor did they keep us long in waiting; for before we had had time to run out fully in our minds this parallel between the two most wonderful agents of the present century, we found ourselves at the Relay House. Here we were joined by old Genl. Hailes and lady of Cincinnati, and in five minutes were off again for the City of Monuments. We reached the outer depot at a quarter past two, having come from Washington in an hour and a half; and now in the midst of forges, engines and workshops, we were surrounded by a multitude of those hardy sons of toil, who constitute so large a portion of our country's glory. They were out in no holiday garments and with no pomp of ceremony, but with beaming eyes, with many forms, with stout arms and honest hearts, with the marks upon their persons which proclaimed their honorable industry and surrounded alike by the instruments and the results of their successful labor. Glorious as are the achievements of human skill, man after all has produced nothing half so wonderful as himself, for God made *him* after his own image. The President must have been gratified with the cordial reception given him at this depot, and have hailed it as a bright omen for his future journey.

He was called from the greetings of the crowd by the entrance of the Mayor of Baltimore, Col Daveis, who introduced to him Messrs. Hack, Spurrier, Colton, Walsh, Stansbury and Ninde, of the Corporation Committee; and after Mrs Polk and Miss Rucker had been taken to their lodgings in a closed carriage, he was seated in an elegant barouche, and with the Mayor and Mr Clifford, was drawn to the line of his reception by the military. The others of his party followed in separate barouches, in each of which were some of the members of the City Committee. His approach had been announced by a salute of twenty one guns, and a brilliant escort was in readiness to receive him. The troops were drawn up on the east side of Hanover Street, with the right resting on Baltimore Street, and composed upwards of twenty companies, attended by their respective bands of music, and all under the efficient command of General George W. Stewart. The President was received into line from Lombard Street, and the procession immediately advanced by Baltimore Street to Gay, where the line was again formed, when the President passed down to the Exchange Hotel. During the progress of the procession through the Streets, banners were waving in all directions, and besides the multitude which thronged the pavements, the windows on every side were filled with spectators. The President gracefully bowed his thanks, as he passed on, and reached the end of the route arranged for him, just in time to avoid a drenching shower, which, refreshing as it was after the heat of the day, would have been any thing but pleasant had it made its appearance a half hour before.

Arrived at the hotel, the President was escorted into the drawing room by the members of the City Corporation, where he was welcomed to the City by Mayor Daveis in the following address:

Mr President. It affords me the highest gratification to welcome you in the name of the citizens of Baltimore, upon this your first visit to our City, since, by the voice of a free people, you have been chosen the Chief Magistrate of the Republic, and to tender to you, Sir, as I now do, the hospitalities of the City, most freely and cordially, during your sojourn among us. The people of Baltimore have, upon all occasions, when the opportunity has been afforded them, not been backward in the expression of their appreciation of such of their fellow citizens whose lives have been devoted to the true glory and prosperity of their country, either in the field or the Cabinet; and most happy are they, on the present occasion, to greet you, Sir, and exchange congratulations, as American citizens may well do, upon the prosperous condition of our beloved Country, and the brilliant prospects which await her future destiny. I renew again, Sir, the assurance, in the name of the whole people, that the citizens of Baltimore esteem themselves happy to welcome you as their distinguished guest, and most gladly will they embrace the opportunity of testifying, in person, the warmth of their regard, and their profound respect for you, Sir, the honored head of a united people.

The President replied:

Sir, I acknowledge gratefully the kind reception I have met with today among the people of Baltimore, and the tender of the hospitalities of the City, which you have now made as the organ of the municipal authorities. I have, indeed, been welcomed in the most gratifying manner, to one of the most beautiful and interesting cities in our whole country, renowned as it has been in our history, as the Monumental City, by the memorials of the gallant achievements of her sons. In the presence of so much hospitality and courtesy, I feel myself in the society of my countrymen and in the home of friends. I have long desired to visit you, but it has not before been convenient for me to do so. After more than two years of almost constant confinement and of unremitting attention to my responsible public duties, I have availed myself of the present occasion when I have reason to suppose I can, without detriment to the public service, be absent for a few days from the Seat of Government. The purpose of my brief visit is to pay my respects to my fellow citizens of Baltimore and of the northern section of this country. Had I postponed it beyond the present summer, it is not probable that any other convenient opportunity to make it, would have occurred, during the period of my term of official service, at the close of which I shall retire to private life. And I hope, Sir, to retire, leaving the administration of my country in the hands of a worthy successor, and that country which has honored me so much, I trust to commit to that successor prosperous and happy.

The reply was appropriate and impressively delivered; but it would have been much more effective, had it been spoken in the animating presence of a crowd. The President should have been addressed in the open air, face to face with the great multitude, and then his response would have derived fresh energy and power by the circumstances which surrounded him. True eloquence is tumultuous in its very nature, and shrinks from quiet and retirement, as from an atmosphere which it cannot breathe in safety. In this instance, too, the Speaker was not a man who could be embarrassed by the vastness of his audience, but one rather who, from his previous habits in the West, as well as from the character of his mind, would have felt far more at home in addressing a popular assembly, than he could possibly feel while addressing a score of persons in a private apartment of the Exchange. The Baltimoreans were mistaken, therefore, in compelling him thus quietly to acknowledge their most honorable reception, but the mistake originated in the best intentions, and was the only one which could be discovered in all the liberal arrangements by which they marked the occasion of the President's visit.

The addresses having been concluded, the President passed at once into the Rotunda of the Exchange, where he received the citizens generally; and from three to five o'clock, they continued to pass before him in one uninterrupted concourse, all anxious to pay the appropriate tribute of respect to the Chief Magistrate of their nation. The various military companies of the city also paid him their personal respects, their officers being severally introduced by the Mayor. At 5 o'clock he retired to his own apartment, but was almost immediately called back to the Rotunda by the arrival of the venerable Association of the Defenders of Baltimore in 1814. Gen. Miltenberger, President of the Association, was presented to him by Col. Daveis, and after him the other members were severally introduced. One of them, J. C. Stapleton, expressed their gratification at meeting him in Baltimore, and feelingly referred to the kind reception given them at the Presidential mansion during their visit to Washington, on the twelfth of September 1845. The reply of the President was truly eloquent. He acknowledged the high honor done him by the visit of so venerable and patriotic a Society, and rejoiced that, as they were passing from the Stage of Life, they had given him an opportunity to meet so many of them in the beautiful city for whose defence they had formerly put in peril their lives. The deeds and the heroes of the last war could never fail to awaken the deepest interest and gratitude in the heart of every American who is worthy of his country; and recent events had demonstrated that the spirit of noble ancestors was still alive in the bosoms of their sons, and that the latter were ready and able to preserve what their fathers had successfully defended. He wished the members of the Association all happiness and repose during the remainder of their lives, and again assured them that he regarded their unexpected visit as an honor done him of the most gratifying character.

Immediately after the Defenders, came the scholars of the Female High School, and part of Female Public School No. 3, accompanied by their teachers, and Messrs. Wilson, Boyd and Dr Monmonier, of the Board of School Commissioners. Mr Boyd introduced the pupils in the following words:

Mr President. It affords me much pleasure to introduce to you the scholars of the Eastern Female High School of Baltimore City. These young ladies, influenced by that patriotic devotion to the institutions of our country which seems to possess our entire community, have presented themselves to pay their respects to its Chief Magistrate. I will not on this occasion tax your time and patience with a detail of the history of our public schools, or scholars. Suffice it to say, that a system of public schools is permanently established in our city, sustained by contributions from our citizens in the shape of "school tax," which is most cheerfully and promptly paid. All admit it to be the most profitable investment the city has made; and as the budding of some of its fruits, allow me to present to you Miss Mathiott, one of the scholars, who will speak for her associates.

Miss Mathiott then presented his Excellency a most superb bouquet, accompanied by the following address:

Mr President, amidst the congratulations of your fellow citizens will you permit the pupils of the Eastern Female High School to tender you a most cordial welcome to Baltimore. Your Excellency, in travelling through this wide and happy land, requires no armed guards, as do the princes and rulers of other countries, for your protection; the affections of a free people will always be the best safeguard of their President. Welcome, then, renowned Sir, to the City of Monuments, to the city that gives graves to its invaders, and honors to its defenders, to the city that feeds the hungry and clothes the naked, and to a city that is training up its youth in knowledge and in virtue. Being well aware that public education has your countenance and influence, as the best means of perpetuating civil and religious liberty to generations yet unborn, we ask you to accept this bouquet as a small token of our sincere and profound respect.

The President had only time to return his thanks for this interesting mark of respect, when he was interrupted by the Junior Artillery, Capt. Gill, who had called to make their personal salutations, and who soon after took their leave. After this presentation, he again retired, alike gratified and weary.

At half after six the President and company (except the ladies who had already dined) were conducted to dinner. The mayor presided at the tables, and the Council and Committees, with many invited guests, were present. Among the distinguished guests were Hon Lewis McLane, Hon. Reverdy Johnson, Judges Heath and Legrand, General Stewart, Commodore Ridgeley, and Attorney Genl. Richardson. The dinner was admirable and admirably served, and the wines were generous enough to attract notice. The whole entertainment passed off joyously, and the company separated in the best of spirits.

About eight o'clock the President again received the visits of the citizens, who poured in upon him in a dense crowd for upwards of an hour, and who were still coming when at half past nine, he felt himself obliged to retire. Meanwhile Mrs Polk and Miss Rucker were receiving a few of their friends in a private parlor, where a very agreeable circle continued until near eleven o'clock.

The day was closed by a serenade from the splendid band of the Independent Blues; and then, in preparation for an early departure the next morning, the whole party retired to rest.

The afternoon had passed off in the happiest manner, and the people of Baltimore deserve great credit for the cordiality as well as elegance with which they received the Chief Magistrate of their Country. Such a reception was in strict accordance with their established reputation for hospitality and patriotism. On several previous occasions within a brief period, they had been called upon for extensive civic and military displays; but they, nevertheless, abated nothing towards the present occasion, either of liberality or grace. I was glad to observe that the City was manifestly increasing both in numbers and in wealth, and we, all of us, I am sure, left with it our best wishes for its continued prosperity and welfare. Its position is favorable to an extensive and profitable trade; and its citizens seem determined to pursue their advantages with zeal and industry. Already the great market for Maryland and a large section of Pennsylvania, it is still extending its avenues of internal commerce, and is grasping now after the exhaustless products of the giant West. Since the time of President Monroe, she has nearly doubled her population, and she is as large as Philadelphia was then. The President who shall visit her twenty years hence, will be welcomed by a population of a hundred and fifty thousand, and still she will be pressing on, we trust, to fill the measure of her affluent success. This is one of the peculiar glories of America, that wherever we pursue our pathway within her borders, we need have no fear of discovering the signs of ruin or the mournful monuments of decay, but we rejoice, on the contrary, to see plenty and abundance flowing on every side, the healthy glow of rewarded industry and the vigorous promise of elastic youth. Great as she is in the present, our Country is greater yet "by the all-hail *hereafter*," and while older nations regret the past and mourn over the threatening evils of the present, America presses forward, with undoubting confidence, to the rising grandeurs of her distant future.

Wednesday June 23

[Departure Baltimore]

At half past 6 o'clock A.M. the President and his party were at the breakfast table, and at 7 o'clock were taken in carriages to a special train of cars for Wilmington (Delaware). Mrs Polk and Miss Rucker were left behind to pursue their way with Mr Russworm, to Tennessee, where they were sure to find a reception as warm and as friendly as any which could be given to the President at the North. Had they continued with us, they would have been every where greeted in the most gratifying and cordial manner, for along the whole line of our journey, the friends of the President were earnest and sincere in regretting the absence of his honored lady. Yet considering the rapidity with which we travelled, and the fatigues which necessarily marked our route, the arrangement was doubtless wise which compelled us to separate from Mrs Polk at Baltimore.

But we were off for Wilmington, and amid cheers and gratulations as we advanced, the President was safely landed in that ancient City a little after ten o'clock. Mr Spurrier of the Baltimore Committee, Judge Pettit, Col. Leiper, Col. Forney, Dr Kane and others, of Philadelphia, accompanied us. "The Doctor," of the Herald, had now joined us, also, and faithfully reported the President's progress and receptions throughout our entire journey.

On reaching the depot at Wilmington the President was greeted with enthusiastic cheers from a vast concourse of its assembled citizens; and at the same time a hoarse welcome to the City's guest was thundered forth from the guns of the Revenue Cutter "Crawford," which was then riding in the harbor, under the command of Capt. Robert Day. Before the salute of twenty-one guns was ended, he entered a barouche provided for him, and accompanied by his Suite, and the Committee of reception from Philadelphia, and followed by a large number of carriages and citizens, proceeded on a tour through the City, going up French St. to 8th, up 8th to King, up King to the Brandywine bridge, from the Bridge down Market St. to the City Hall, where we entered, by invitation of the Mayor and Council. The President was here welcomed by Col. Samuel B. Davis, a gentleman over eighty years of age, formerly a member of the House of Representatives of Pennsylvania from Philadelphia, and a distinguished officer during the last war with England. He said he was glad to have the opportunity of welcoming so illustrious a guest, and took pleasure in offering him the civilities of Wilmington. The President replied, that he was unable to speak at length. He was deeply gratified with the enthusiastic reception, which had been given him in this interesting city, and had great satisfaction in meeting, on the occasion, the venerable gentleman by whom he had now been addressed. He was rejoiced to see the evidences of prosperity around him. They were to be attributed, not to the measures of his Administration, but to the vigor and energy of a free people; yet he none the less regarded them with interest and gratitude. He trusted they would never be found wanting in the State of Delaware, but would multiply rather, and illustrate her increasing growth and rising prosperity.

After exchanging salutations with the citizens in the hall below (among whom were Mr Hicks, Collector of Wilmington, and Mr Chandler, Editor of the Gazette) the President and Suite, with the Philadelphia Committee and others, were invited upstairs to partake of a bountiful collation which had been provided by the Mayor and Council. The collation finished, the procession again formed, and proceeded to the Steamer, which had been provided by the Philadelphians to convey the party to the "Quaker City." This was the "George Washington," a fine boat, decorated for the occasion in good taste and accompanied by the excellent band of the State Fencibles. She had come from Philadelphia during the forenoon, and among those whom she brought with her to welcome the President, were Col. James Page, Collector, Dr Geo. F. Lehman, Postmaster, Genl. Geo. M. Keim, Marshall, Hon. J. K. Kane, Dist. Judge, Thos. M. Pettit, Dist. Attorney, Henry Welsh, Naval Officer, Henry Lelar, Sheriff, Genl. John Davis, Surveyor, Prof. R. M. Patterson, Director of the Mint, Hon. John T. Smith, Col. T. B. Florence, Col. James Goodman, Geo. Plitt, Wm. Badger, Robt. Ewing, Robt. F. Christy, Judge Champneys, Atty Genl., Col. J. R. Snowden, Treasurer of the Mint, Col. Patterson, Navy Agent, Recorder R. M. Lee, Geo. Sheetz, of Montgomery, 83 years of age, & three times Elector for Gen. Jackson, Gen. N. Raney, of St. Louis, Maj. Hurst, and a large number of representatives of the press, including Fulton, of the Ledger, Bell, of the Gazette, Wood, of the North American, Church, of the Bulletin, and Blackburn, of the Times.

The Steamer was under way at twenty minutes before twelve, amid cheers from the crowd, music from the band, and another salute of twenty one guns from the Cutter "Crawford." The succeeding half hour was taken up in introducing to the President the Committees of Wilmington and Philadelphia, and the accompanying gentlemen. Following these presentations came the dinner, when about one hundred persons sat down at dinner, and did ample justice to the sumptuous repast which had been prepared for the occasion on board the "Washington."

The company having returned to the deck, and the boat about crossing the line that divides Pennsylvania and Delaware, W. H. Rogers Esq in behalf of the latter State, made a short and happy address in resigning his guest to the charge of the Pennsylvania Committee, consisting of the Hon. Benja. Champneys, Wm. Badger, Robert Ewing, Frederic Stoever and Saml. D. Patterson. Judge Champneys then welcomed the President into the Keystone State in a highly appropriate and interesting manner. Both these addresses had been suitably prepared, and were in excellent taste, but they were far exceeded by the reply of the President, both in eloquence of thought and in power of delivery. They elicited the most brilliant response which the President made throughout his journey; and yet so completely was his audience taken by surprise, that no one among them thought to take notes of it for publication. There were several Reporters present, but they actually forgot their pens and listened, and as the finest eloquence, like the most precious perfumes, are usually the most difficult to preserve, no worthy account of the President's remarks on this occasion, has yet been secured. As they were concluded, the boat was rapidly approaching Old Chester. The wharf, which extends into the river from that patriotic town, was crowded with its citizens, of either sex, while about thirty yards in the rear, along the river's bank, were drawn up in military array, some twenty-five or thirty men, in their shirt sleeves and strawhats, and each with a musket on his shoulder. They fired numerous rounds by way of salute, and they themselves, together with Judge Leiper, their leader, were repeatedly cheered, by the delighted spectators on board the steamer.

The Washington arrived off the Navy Yard about ten minutes past two o'clock, accompanied from Gloucester by the steamers "Stranger" and "Fashion," and one of the new government propellers, gaily dressed off with innumerable flags, and filled with citizens anxious to catch even a passing glimpse of the

President. The boat moved on up the river as far as the Dyottville glass works; then turned about and came to at the Navy Yard about three o'clock. The wharves all along the City's front, and the shipping (all of which had flags flying to the breeze) were crowded with people, who cheered enthusiastically, as our gallant steamer pursued her way. Meanwhile our friends in Jersey as well as in Philadelphia made the welkin ring with oft-repeated thunder from their well-managed ordnance; and heavy reports, also, from the Cutter Forward, just above the Navy Yard, gave life and animation to the scene.

At ten minutes past three o'clock, the President and Suite, and the Philadelphia Committee of Arrangements, landed at the Navy Yard Wharf, under a national salute, and met with a glorious reception. The Yard itself, the tops of houses, the streets, lanes and alleys, in the vicinity of the landing, were crowded with thousands of eager spectators, all intent upon seeing and honoring the distinguished head of their Country. He was received by Commodore Stewart, Commandant of the Yard, Maj. Gen. Patterson, Col. Abercrombie, and several other officers of the Army and Navy. He was then preceded by a handsome military escort and conducted to the quarters of Commodore Stewart, in the Navy Yard, where the whole party did full justice to a handsome collation.

At half after four o'clock, the military had formed under the admirable direction of Gen. Roumfort, and the procession proceeded on its designated route the City. The way was led by a splendid brigade (the 1st) consisting of a troop of cavalry, a regiment of artillery, and a regiment of infantry, with bands of music at appropriate intervals. Then followed the President, with the Hon. John K. Kane, Ch. of the Reception Committee, in a barouche drawn by four white horses. Next came twelve barouches, each with four horses attached, containing the Suite of the President, various distinguished guests, and the various Committees of the City and County of Philadelphia. Fifteen carriages followed with the Committees from Wilmington and other places, and three troops of cavalry next formed a body guard, and presented a fine appearance. The rear guard was composed of three brigades of artillery and infantry, and the procession was closed by a long array of mounted citizens. Around the City and through the City, from Southwark to Spring Garden, and back again to the Eastward, we now extended our circuitous line of march, affording an excellent view of the President in his open barouche to the thousands upon thousands who filled the sidewalks and windows, all the way, for the purpose of seeing him. After a march of nearly three hours, we paused at last, at the residence of Vice President Dallas, in Walnut Street, into which the President was conducted with his official Suite. An immense multitude now blocked up the street in the neighborhood of the house, and, first, the President, and, afterwards, Gen. Patterson, was loudly called for. Mr Dallas appeared upon the threshhold, and apologizing for the inability of the President, after his great fatigue, to address them then, informed them that he would be happy to meet them the next day at Independence Hall. Gen. Patterson, he said, was always ready in the battlefield, but he was a man of deeds rather than words and desired on this occasion to be excused. The crowd (and a majestic one it was) soon after dispersed; and leaving the President to the hospitalities of Mr Dallas, Mr Clifford, Mr Burke, and Mr Appleton were conducted to their respective rooms at Jones's. In the evening, the President was serenaded by the "Breiter Association" and the "Maennerchor."

His whole route today, from Wilmington and through the streets of Philadelphia, was marked by the most pleasing indications of general hospitality and joy. The shores of the Delaware, and all the avenues of the City were filled with people, and the roar of cannon, the cheers of the citizens, the crowded wharves and shipping, and the brilliant display of the military, made the scene one of singular animation and interest. Commodore Stewart, who had witnessed the receptions of LaFayette and Jackson, declared that, in his opinion, neither of them was equal to this. It would hardly, indeed, be otherwise; for since Old Hickory's journey, Philadelphia has largely increased her population and added to her wealth. In the year 1830 she numbered a hundred and sixty seven thousand inhabitants, and she now has about two hundred and thirty thousand. The difference indicates her general advancement, and would lead us to anticipate other things being equal, a more brilliant reception from her citizens

to every succeeding President. Yet it is creditable to any Chief
Magistrate that he is enabled so to command the respect of a large
City, as to receive from its population, a reception as magnificent
as that which was given to President Polk, on this occasion, in
Philadelphia. It was equally honorable to the City that at such
a period, its authorities and its people united, without distinction
of party, to extend its most liberal hospitalities to the highest
functionary of the republic.

Thursday June 24

[Tour Philadelphia]

The weather still continued beautiful, and after an early breakfast,
the President and Suite, with the Vice President, Judge Kane,
Gen. Roumfort, Col. Florence, W. J. Leiper Esq, Hon. Mr Smith,
Judge Champneys, and others, proceeded in carriages to visit the
Girard College. Entering the central building and exploring it
from its basement to its massive marble roof, we descended to
the northern Portico, where about a hundred and fifty workmen
were assembled to pay their respects to the Chief Magistrate of
the United States. After an exchange of salutations with this
multitude of the "bone and sinew," we resumed our carriages,
and the President, on parting, received three hearty cheers.

In point of exterior beauty there is no building probably in
the union, which can surpass the principal structure of the Girard
group, and it is distinguished for strength and stability as well as
for beauty and grace. Its interior arrangements seemed to me ill-
adapted to the purposes of a college, but no one can help admiring
its vast proportions, its elegant architecture and its perfect finish.
I was much struck with the figure which we saw here, of Girard
himself. It is a statue of white marble, the size of life, the work
of a French artist, and represents its original, not in any Roman
or Grecian costume, but in the everyday dress in which he used
constantly to be recognized on the streets of Philadelphia. It is the
most life-like statue I ever saw, and is said to be a most faithful
representation of Mr Girard. To the present generation, at least,

it is in much better taste than if it exhibited the old gentleman in some fanciful drapery of the artist.

From the College We passed over to the Eastern Penitentiary, and were escorted, under direction of Judge Bradford, through one of its principal wings. Each cell seemed to have but one occupant who found relief in some manual employment. We entered a vacant cell which had been occupied by a German, who was not compelled to labor; and in what appeared to be elaborately figured paper upon the walls, we saw one of the modes in which he had whiled away the weary hours of his imprisonment. In the same apartment were exhibited a set of miniature knives and forks, which a subsequent prisoner had carved from bone in the most ingenious manner. Even in the Penitentiary there is no contentment without labor. From the cells we were taken into the receiving room of the warden, where we found refreshments provided, and soon after we returned to the city. A visit to Fairmount Water Works had been proposed, but the President had been increasingly threatened with illness, since he left Baltimore, and he felt obliged now to husband his strength. After he had rested for an hour or two, he was met by the Committee again, and proceeded with his Suite to the "Model School" in Chester Street. This institution is divided into three departments for the boys and girls connected with it, and each department occupies a separate story of the building. The Superintendent, Mr Miller, introduced the President and his friends to the pupils in the several rooms, in a brief strain of appropiate remark. The children in the secondary school joined in a patriotic song of welcome as we entered, and in a similar manner, as we departed, bade us adieu. In the boys' grammar division, Master George Alvord welcomed the President in a complimentary address to which the President replied in suitable terms of kindness and admonitions. In the girls' department Miss Eliza Y. Bodine, after the general introduction, passed up to the President, and modestly curtesying, presented him with a large bouquet of rare and elegant flowers.

From the "Model School" we went to the Central High School for boys, near the Mint, and under the charge of John S. Hart. This school numbers some four hundred pupils, distributed in numerous apartments, to all of which we were permitted to make only a flying visit, for the time had already gone by when we were to be at the U.S. Mint.

To the Mint we were now conducted, where we were introduced to Professor Patterson, Director, Col. Snowden, Treasurer, and other gentlemen connected with its various arrangements. The want of time did not permit us to see it as we could have wished, but we spent a half hour there with the greatest pleasure and interest. The departments of the institution were, all of them, in full operation, and we saw the raw metal taken through all the processes, of melting, casting, rolling, clipping, cutting, edging, stamping and washing. The ingots of silver, straps of gold, cauldrons of boiling wealth, tubs of eagles and dollars, made a most princely display of hard money, while the machinery by which it was perfected could not fail to attract attention for its beauty and its elegance. The steam-engine was particularly deserving of notice, and every thing about the premises seemed to be in the very best order. Several medals bearing the image of President Polk, and dated 1845 were struck, upon this occasion, from a die previously prepared, and one of them presented to the President, the Vice President, and to each of the President's Suite. The likeness is a good one, and the medal executed with unusual success.

From the Mint the President went to the Old State House, in Independence Square, where he was to receive the people until three o'clock. Here, he was officially welcomed by the Mayor, Mr Swift, in the presence of the City Councils, in a speech which was marked alike by warmth and by propriety. The President replied, thanking the City not only for the distinquished reception it had given him, but also for receiving him in that honored hall. It was a place consecrated by the memories of the Hancocks, the Adamses, the Jeffersons and all the immortal fathers of our independence, and he could not visit it, as he now did, for the first time, without emotions of the most interesting character. It carried him back to the beginning of our revolutionary struggle, and to all the toil and peril and suffering to which that struggle led. It was instinct, too, with lessons of patriotic wisdom, for amid recollections like those which there crowded on the mind, no American could entertain a thought of sectional feeling or party strife, or hesitate in his full and devoted regard for our beloved Union. Adverting, then, to the motives which were found in the extended prosperity and growth of our country, for increased fidelity to its invaluable institutions, he closed by again thanking the gentlemen of the Corporation for their kind and cordial welcome. There was, then, a general introduction of visitors to the President, which continued until past three o'clock, when he returned to Mr Dallas's for a little rest.

At 5 o'clock, the President and Suite, with the Mayor, Comd. Stewart, Genl. Patterson, Judge Kane, Mr Randall, Professor Patterson, Hon J. R. Ingersoll, Hon. Chas. Brown and others, sat down at an elegant dinner with the Vice President. The entertainment passed off in the happiest manner, and at its close, the President was hurried off, under charge of Mr Brown, to see the assembled people in the Northern Liberties. Mr Brown introduced him to the multitude, but many of them insisted upon taking him by the hand, while the cheers which saluted him were almost uproarious, and the whole reception "rather too exciting to be pleasant." He made his escape as soon as possible, and, calling at the Democratic Headquarters as he returned, reached his lodgings in season to prepare for the princely levee of Genl. Patterson which closed the festivities of the day. The General has an elegant mansion, and on this occasion, it was elegantly filled, female beauty and military display striving for preeminence. The President excused himself from this brilliant scene at an early hour, and sought from his pillow that repose which he so much needed. At midnight he was again serenaded, and with music such as the most weary votary of sleep would be compelled alike to pardon and to praise.

In Philadelphia, the President received invitations to attend all the public exhibitions of the place, and urgent requests to visit several towns in the interior, but he was compelled to decline them all; and pursued steadily his original route.

The young gentlemen from Tennessee separated from us after our arrival in the Quaker City; but Commodore Stewart, in return, was added to our party, and continued with the President throughout his journey. Though upwards of seventy years of age, "Old Ironsides" yet proved himself vigorous and strong, and bore all the fatigues of the tour as lightly as any one of the company. In the New England States, where he is almost a stranger, he was an object of great attraction to the people, who remembered that however old he might be now, he once had a "Constitution" stronger than the united force of two British Sloops.

Friday June 25

[Departure Philadelphia]

At seven o'clock in the morning, the Philadelphia Committee called at "Jones's" for the gentlemen composing the President's Suite, and they were taken in carriages to the mansion of the Vice President. Here after a quarter of an hour spent in leave-taking, the President was received, and the carriages then passed down Walnut Street to the ferry. We were accompanied from Philadelphia by Col. Florence, Col. Christie, Mr Stewart, and Col. Leiper, of that city, by Genl. Wall, Hon. J. R. Thompson, Capt. C. A. Stevens, J. S. Green Esq, Col. Wm. Cook, Dr Arnold, Col. Nelson, and Capt. Mickle, of New Jersey, and by Aldermen Crolius, Purser, and Stevens, of New York.

Having crossed the Delaware, the President was received at Camden by a salute of artillery, and by a large assembly of the people of that time, in whose behalf, Capt. Mickle addressed him as follows:

Mr President, I am happy in the opportunity of welcoming you to the State of New Jersey. We bid you welcome, not only as President of the United States, but individually we bid you welcome. We trust, Sir, that the prosperity of the country, never greater than at present, may continue, and that the war which has been forced upon us by the enemy, may be ended as it has begun, in a blaze of glory. Again, Sir, we welcome you to our State. May your passage over it be safe and pleasant and may you return to your family in health and happiness.

The President, in reply, returned his thanks for the cordial welcome which had been given him to New Jersey. He was rejoiced to hear of her prosperous condition, and hoped that she might still continue to advance in every thing which tended to her substantial wealth and her real glory. He regretted that his engagements did not permit him to remain longer among her citizens, and hoped that he might have an opportunity, on his return, to make them a longer visit. We then took our seats in the cars and proceeded slowly through the village. As the train (a special one) advanced, some thirty young ladies, tastefully dressed, stood along the sidewalk in a line, waving their white handkerchiefs, and looking their happy welcomes to the Chief Magistrate of the Nation. They were intended to represent the several states and territories of the Union, and would as such have been presented, had time allowed, to the President. But we were obliged to avoid all delay.

Passing rapidly on (the locomotive gaily decorated with flags) we saw the residence of Mrs Bradford, daughter of Elias Boudinot, that of Bishop Doane, and that of Joseph Bonaparte, while nature presented a delightful appearance in the grain crops and peach orchards all along the way. At Bordentown there was a full turnout of citizens, among whom were the workmen from the neighboring foundries, and there the President was most heartily and repeatedly cheered. An old fashioned piece of artillery, two drawn up near the road, was kept on constant duty, in honor of the Presidential visit. At Burlington and Hightstown, there were similar demonstrations of welcome, and at the latter place, we were joined by Hon. J. A. Wright and Hon. George Sykes.

We reached South Amboy at 1/2 past 10 o'clock, having come so rapidly as to anticipate the arrival of the steamer (the Cornelius Vanderbilt) which was to take us to New York. We passed out of the cars to a public house near by, which, homely enough in itself, had yet a delightful location. On a pleasant green in its front, the Mayor of the place, with a committee, met the President and exchanged with him appropriate salutations. Soon after, the steamer "Eureka" arrived from New York, and a long procession came up from it, attended by a band of music, and composed of various committees from the empire city, headed respectively by R. H. Maclay, W. McMurray, and D. C. Broderick Esq. Mr Maclay made an animated speech of welcome, and received an equally earnest and appropriate reply. The procession then returned to the boat, after a round of hearty cheers, and shortly after, the "Vanderbilt" having arrived, the President and his party resumed their seats in the cars, and were taken immediately to the landing. At this point Alderman Oliver addressed him, and informed him that the Council of New York was in waiting to bid him welcome to the Commercial Emporium of the Union. Genl. Wall next took leave of him in behalf of New Jersey. He spoke of the heartiness of her welcome, the hospitality of her people, her increasing prosperity, her revolutionary services, her attachment to the Union, and expressed the hope, that, after a prosperous journey North, the President might be able, on his return, to pass a longer time within her borders. To both of these addresses the President replied with great energy and warmth; but owing to the neighborhood of the "Vanderbilt," which was letting off steam, it was impossible to gather a connected account of his remarks. As soon as they were concluded, he was conducted on board the boat.

The "Vanderbilt" is one of the most swift and elegant of the New York Steamers, and on this occasion she was in charge of Captain Vanderbilt himself. She had on board the members of the New York Council, and about five hundred invited guests, among whom were represented the army and navy, the bench and the bar, diplomacy and commerce. The President here met his brother, the Chargé to Naples. It was a great crowd, but everybody was in good humor, and there was no disorder or scarcely even a breach of courtesy. The arrangements of the committee had been admirable, and they were thoroughly carried into effect. Refreshments of all kinds were found on board the boat, and we had in company a fine band of music. The New Yorkers were hospitable on this occasion in a manner worthy of their city.

When the President reached the upper saloon of the boat, he was addressed by Morris Franklin Esq, President of the Board of Aldermen, who, in behalf of the City Councils, assured him of a hearty reception in the great emporium of New York. He spoke in substance as follows:

Mr President. On behalf of the Common Council of the City of New York, and in accordance with my feelings, I most respectfully tender to you a sincere and cordial welcome upon your approach to the commercial emporium of our country, and in so doing I but speak the united sentiments of my fellow citizens, without regard to sect or party. For it is indeed an imposing and interesting spectacle, to see in the midst of a free, prosperous and independent people, the representative whom they have elected to occupy the highest office within the gift of man; and thousands upon thousands are now assembled in anxious expectations of extending the right hand of fellowship to so illustrious and distinguished a stranger. You are about to enter a city, which, but a century and a half ago, contained only four thousand, three hundred inhabitants, but which now numbers within its borders four hundred thousand souls, who mingle together in their daily avocations with a spirit of harmony and natural forbearance, indicative of the beauty of our institutions, and the blessings of a liberal and enlightened government. And, although we cannot, if we would, receive you with the pomp and splendor of European magnificence (for we are a plain, democratic and domestic people) yet we can and do bid you welcome from the overflowings of patriotic and grateful hearts for the liberal dispensations of an overruling and bountiful Providence. We can introduce you, Sir, to one of the noblest harbors of the world, where ride in perfect safety the ships of every clime, and where float upon every breeze the national emblems of commercial intercourse. We can present to you institutions, fostered and encouraged by the protecting care of a philanthropic Government, where poverty and disease receive protection and relief, where the deaf and the dumb, the orphan and the blind, without regard to age, nativity or color, are the objects of our sympathy and regard. Upon our public streets and retired avenues, rise in majestic splendor temples dedicated to our holy religion, whose towering spires, capped with the emblem of the Christian's faith, point in silent grandeur to the object of our worship, and tend to remind the passing traveller of the gate to Heaven. There, too, may be seen extensive halls consecrated to literature and science, and although it has been said that Mammon is the God of our idolatry, yet there are those who love to worship at these shrines and dwell within their holy influences. But, the crowning monument of our City's enterprise, is that noble aqueduct which, from a source of fifty miles distributes within our midst the pure exhilarating contents of the Croton Lake, affording protection in time of danger, and a delightful beverage to all.

But, Sir, I need not dwell upon matters such as these, for you are now with us as our guest, and as time and opportunity are afforded, it will be our pleasure to present for your consideration such objects as may be worthy of your interest and attention: and in the meanwhile, I again repeat that you are welcome, thrice welcome to the hospitalities of our city.

The President replied:

For this cordial welcome which you give, Sir, on my approach to your great city, I can only express my deep gratitude and satisfaction. I know, Sir, that the distinguished attentions which you proffer me, are rendered to the station which I have the honor to hold (the highest, as you have Justly said, in the gift of man) and not the individual who holds it. As such I receive them and respond to them, and with gratification all the deeper, because they proceed from no party, but from my fellow-citizens generally. I regard this, Sir, as an occasion of deep interest and pleasure, because it strikingly illustrates that fundamental truth of our institutions, that freemen are competent to elect their own rulers, and are not dependent upon the divine right, which in most other countries, is considered as the only source of legitimate authority. In the high office which I hold, I am the representative only of the American people, and in that capacity, it has been by earnest endeavor so to conduct the important affairs entrusted to me as to be found no unworthy occupant of the place in which so many illustrious men have preceded me; and I devoutly trust that guided ever by a deep sense of obligation to my country, I may be enabled, at the close of my official term, to leave that country to my Successor, alike prosperous at home and respected abroad.

It will give me great pleasure, Sir, to visit your public works and to behold the evidences of your wealth and enterprise. Your vast improvements are not unknown to me, but I shall derive new satisfaction from inspecting them under your guidance. I shall be rejoiced, also, to observe your benevolent institutions and to appreciate the extent and munificence of those charities which adorn and ennoble this Commercial Metropolis. In the City of New York, we have a representation of the whole republic, and from its prosperity some idea may be formed of the power and resources of the nation. The extent of those resources can as yet only be imagined; but if our countrymen are true to their free institutions and to their invaluable Union, there is nothing in the future of grandeur and of glory, which we may not anticipate for our beloved country. Already we have increased, within little more than half a century, from four millions to twenty millions, but he who shall live to see the President of the United States, fifty years hence, will welcome the representative of a hundred millions of people.

Permit me, Sir, in conclusion, to renew to you and to your associates of the Common Council, my hearty thanks for the very agreeable manner in which you have offered me the hospitalities of New York.

The ceremony of introduction was now commenced, but before the guests had been all presented, the President was obliged to retire to one of the cabins for repose. He had been ill ever since he left Baltimore, and it is surprising how, under such circumstances, he was enabled to sustain himself so well. Yet he rarely lost his animation, and in his occasional addresses always spoke with effect.

He had scarcely more than half an hour's rest before he was summoned below to dinner, and the entertainment which we met in the saloon, considering its extent and the place of its preparation, was certainly as elegant and bounteous, as any which I had ever witnessed before. The tables were literally loaded with every thing which could delight the palate, and the richest wines were provided in unmeasured abundance. Numerous and practised attendants prevented all confusion at the tables, and the dinner passed off as agreeably and with as little discomfort as if it had been furnished in one of the spacious halls of the Astor House.

When we again reached the deck, we found we were approaching the bay, and we passed in quick succession, ships, steamers, pilotboats and other vessels who saluted us with bells, guns and cheers. At Perth Amboy, a large number of people were waiting on the dock, and as we passed, they gave us three cheers, fired several guns, and the ladies waved handkerchiefs in profusion while, here and there, groups of children were seen upon the beach, dancing in very joy at their good fortune, in being permitted to see the boat which had the President on board. The Steamer "Eureka" which went ahead of the "Vanderbilt" to Amboy, had cannon on board, and fired a salute from its forward deck. The Steamer "Zephyr" also came down with a swarm of passengers, and after exchanging salutes with the "Vanderbilt," dropped astern, in honor of the President, whom we carried. The Coney Island boat, American Eagle, also came down the bay to meet us, and thus do honor to the President's approach.

As we drew near the City, the President appeared upon the forward deck and introductions were resumed. But the attention of all was soon arrested by the report of heavy guns, and it was discovered the Fort Hamilton had commenced firing its national Salute. As we passed Governor's Island the same compliment was expressed by the ordnance at that place, and the firing now became general, from the revenue cutters in the harbor, from the foreign ships of war, from some of the merchant vessels, and the animating sounds were echoed from every side. The artillery on the battery, too, began to lend their aid, and a continuous roar of cannon ushered the approach of the President to the great City of New York. The vessels, besides, had all their banners out; flags of all nations were flying from hundreds of ships, and from numerous flagstaffs in the neighborhood of the Battery. Among others, a beautiful French banner was exhibited at the foot of Broadway, by the French Steamship Company. Altogether, the display was most brilliant.

It was nearly three o'clock when we reached the landing place at Castle Garden, amid cheers and salutes from every quarter. The battery was alive with people, and it required no small exertion to secure an unobstructed passage through the crowd for the President and his friends. Having reached the platform provided for the introduction, the President was addressed by the Mayor of the city, Wm. Brady Esq, as follows.

The reception of The Chief Executive Officer of the United States is an honor which I duly appreciate, and it affords me great satisfaction, as well for myself as on behalf of the Municipal Authorities and in the name of the citizens of New York, to tender you, Mr President, a cordial welcome to our city. The visit of the President of the United States is always hailed with pleasure in every section of our Country; and it is one of the most gratifying proofs of the influence of our free and enlightened institutions that upon such an occasion as this, all political feelings and prejudices are cast aside, and all seem animated by the sole desire to pay that tribute of respect and esteem which is due to so exalted a position. We are pleased, Sir, to have it in our power to extend to you these attentions and courtesies which, we trust may serve to render your sojourn among us one of equal interest and pleasure, and one which you may have cause to remember hereafter with gratifying emotions. The Common Council of our City have made such arrangements for your examination of our public works and institutions, as your time and convenience will allow.

Permit me, Sir, to introduce to you your fellow citizens, and to assure you that, as well for myself as for them, that nothing shall be wanting on our part to show that the City of New York knows how to receive and to respect the highest officer of our Republic.

After the President had briefly responded to this address, he proceeded to the Battery where he reviewed, on horseback, the long lines of troops. Accompanied, then, by the Mayor and by Aldermen Oliver and Franklin, he was conducted to his carriage (a barouche, and four greys) greeted at almost every step with cheers. He was followed by the Joint Committee of Arrangements, the gentlemen of his *suite*, the members of Common Council of the City, members of Congress and the State Legislature, the Mayors of adjoining Cities and Trustees of Williamsburg, the members of the Society of the Cincinnati, Major General Gaines and Suite, with officers of the Army and Navy, and by Foreign Consuls and members of the Diplomatic Corps, the long line of carriages being closed by those containing the county officers and Officers of the Corporation. This was the First Division of the procession, and was under the direction of Major General Stryker, assisted by Col. H. U. Slipper, and Geo. G. Hopkins Esq, Aids to the Marshal. It contained upwards of fifty carriages, and was escorted by a large Corps of Cavalry.

The Second Division was under the direction of Major Robert B. Boyd, and Captain William H. Cornell. It contained the Society of Tammany, with its beautiful banner, and a splendid band of music, two companies of Light Guards, and, then, the Democratic Republican General Committee and the Democratic Republican Young Men's General Committee, on horseback.

The Third Division was comprised chiefly of members of the Fire Department, in red shirts and glazed caps, and presented a fine appearance.

The last Division consisted of deputations from the various wards of the City and of citizens generally.

Then came the military, General Sandford and Staff, preceded by a splendid band of music, the first brigade of light horse artillery under General Storms, a band of buglers, ushering the New York Hussars, a company of mounted Carbineers, Genl. Morris and Staff, and another company of Hussars. After these

followed the sixth brigade of N.Y. State Artillery, its bands playing Yankee Doodle, then two highland companies, with drum, fife
and bagpipes, then, preceded by a full band, the eighth Light
Infantry, the Washington cadets and the Emmett Guards, then,
the first Light Infantry, the Union Rifles, the Washington Light
Guard, the Montgomery Guards, the Montgomery Light Guards
and the Washington Continental Guards, with their old fashioned
coats, turned up with buff, their yellow breeches, cocked hats, and
white top boots, then, the Light Guard, the Benson Guard, the
Independence Guard, the Italian Guard, the Mechanic Blues, the
Independent Blues, the Lafayette Fusileers and last, the young
Carbineers from Staten Island.

The procession was about two miles long and occupied more
than an hour in passing. The heat of the day was intense, yet the
people were out in all the majesty of numbers, and enthusiasm.
There is no place for a crowd like New York. There seemed to be
a large multitude in Philadelphia, but it was nothing in comparison
with the heaving ocean of humanity upon which we seemed to be
lost in the Empire City. No scene could be more grand and exciting than was presented in Broadway as the procession moved
on. Throughout the entire extent of the line of march, was one
dense mass of human life. Every roof was covered; every win-
dow full of faces, and in doorways, upon steps, in balconies, and
apparently encroaching upon the mid-street itself, near half a million of people seemed to be earnestly intent upon the interesting spectacle. From almost every flagstaff in the city banners
were floating in the breeze; countless handkerchiefs were waving from the hands of ladies and minature streamers were thrust
forth from doorways and casements, on staves supported by the
little hands of childhood. Magnificent bouquets were showered
upon the President's barouche, as it advanced, and cheers and
congratulations were continually outpouring. And at the head of
the pageant, the great object of it all was the Chief Magistrate
of the Union, in plain citizen's dress, with uncovered head, in an
open carriage, and constantly acknowledging the courtesies of his
fellow citizens, as he passed along. In no other nation is such an
exhibition possible.

The procession moved, through continuous crowds, up

Broadway to Astor Place, through Astor Place to the Bowery, and down Chatham Street to the City Hall. Here the President alighted from his carriage, and followed by his *Suite* and various distinguished officers and gentlemen, reviewed the military companies of the procession, and received appropriate Salutes. He then went into the Hall, and walking through the building, was received, in the rear of it, by a carriage, and conveyed directly to his lodgings in the Astor House, where he retired immediately to his room, in order to rest and prepare for dinner. At half past six P.M. we dined. At the table were the President, Mr Clifford, Mr Burke, Mr Appleton, Mr Sykes, Mr W. H. Polk, Captain McKeever, of the Navy, The Mayor, Aldermen Crolius, Franklin, Gray, Purser, Stevens, McKnight, General Wall, J. R. Thompson Esq, Judge Woodworth and R. L. Stevens Esq. The dinner was elegant and was warmly appreciated, for the afternoon had been fatiguing enough to awaken excellent appetites. Soon after dinner, we all sought our respective chambers, and enjoyed that delightful rest which is earned only by exertion. Thus ended the first day in New York, without a single incident which we were compelled to regret, and after a display which was honorable alike to the New Yorkers and to the President.

Saturday June 26

[Tour New York City]

The next morning (Saturday) the President was waited on at six o'clock, by the Mayor and Alderman Oliver, who conducted him in a private carriage, through some portions of the lower City. After having visited the Fulton and Washington Markets (where he was recognized, notwithstanding all his cautions) he accompanied the Mayor to his residence for breakfast, and thence, after a short interval, returned to the Astor House. Here he was introduced to various gentlemen and committees, until the time arrived which had been fixed for receiving the people at the City Hall. At a little after ten o'clock, he repaired to the Governor's Room, attended by Mayor Brady, Aldermen Oliver and Purser, and various members of the Committee of Reception. In this spacious apartment, standing by the writing table of Washington, for nearly two hours, he continued the hard routine of taking by the hand those who crowded unceasingly forward to obtain an introduction. During this period he must have shaken hands with at least two thousand people. Through the excellent arrangements of the Police, only a limited number were admitted to the hall at once, coming in at one door and returning by another, but the pressure without the entrance was almost terrific. The visitors were mingled in true republican style, lawyers, physicians, and divines, *Litterateurs*, merchants, officeholders, and clerks, loafers, and brokers. The well dressed and the *Sans culottes*, all crowded on, in the same dense multitude, and for the same purpose of seeing and knowing their common representative. Females even were there, and young children, among whom a pair of twins were presented to the President, bearing respectively the names of Henry Polk Russell and David Polk Russell.

About eleven o'clock, the officers of the two volunteer regiments, raised nearly a year before for Mexican service, but not yet called for, came in two abreast, headed by Colonel Ming. They formed in open order, facing inwards, and through this avenue passed Mr Polk, leaning upon the arm of Alderman Purser, and giving his hand to each member of the regiment. After the volunteers had retired, the various foreign consuls residing in New York, came forward, in court dresses, to pay their respects, and before he left the Hall, he was waited on by James G. King Esq, Chairman of the Chamber of Commerce, who, in behalf of the Chamber, expressed the gratification which that body felt, in being able to welcome the President of the United States to the Empire City. The President's reply is said to have been one of his happiest efforts, but I was unable to hear it and amid the confusion of the hall it was not reported. During the day, Genl. Morris, B. F. Butler, John McKeon, Theodore Sedgewick, Judge Vanderpoel, R. H. Morris, Cornelius Lawrence and innumerable other gentlemen were presented, and the President only relinquished the duty of reception, when, at twelve o'clock, the time arrived for a flying visit to Brooklyn.

The Brooklyn Committee of Arrangements, The Council of New York and other gentlemen, accompanied him in carriages, after he left the Hall, and he was driven rapidly down Broadway to the Exchange, which he examined for a few minutes, and then proceeded to the Fulton ferry, where he was received with tumultuous shouts by the assembled multitude. Under escort of the Brooklyn Guards, and enlivened by the stirring music of their brass band, he was soon on board the steamer "Wyandauk," which, like the shipping houses in the vicinity, was tastefully decorated with flags and streamers for the occasion. Safely across the river, and saluted with the roar of cannon and the enthusiasm of shouting voices, the President was conducted to his barouche, and was met by the Mayor of Brooklyn, who addressed him as follows:

Mr. President: I have the honor, on behalf of my fellow-citizens, to tender to you a hearty and cordial welcome to the freedom and hospitalities of this city. We feel complimented by your visit, and irrespective of other circumstances, we have assembled to do honor to the Chief Magistrate of the Union. We are aware of the mighty responsibilities which rest on you, of the trials and difficulties you have to encounter in the discharge of your official duties, and we most earnestly implore for you the assistance of the divine Being who rules the destinies of nations, to guide and direct you in administering the affairs of this government, so that great and lasting blessings may rest on our people, and your administration receive the approbation of the virtuous and the good in all coming time. Again, Mr President, I bid you welcome to the civilities and hospitalities of our city.

The President replied:

He was happy in visiting, even for the brief period at his disposal, the beautiful and flourishing city of Brooklyn. His progress thus far on his journey had increased his confidence in the resources of our common country, and in every new spectacle which was presented to him, he found additional proof of her rising glory and advancing prosperity. The allusion which had been made to that overruling Providence, who alone could give him adequate aid in the discharge of his anxious and important duties, had awakened emotions in his mind of peculiar interest. It reminded him that it was to the divine source that all must look in the hour of exigency and peril and doubt. It was this reliance which verved the arms of our fathers in those times which tried men's souls, and which was like the Star of Bethlehem of old, in directing the wise men to the object of their search. He hoped, for himself, always to be able to appreciate its inestimable value, and he hoped, for his country, that such a reliance might always be present in the councils of her highest officers. In conclusion, he begged the citizens of Brooklyn to excuse if he did not remain among them longer than the brief half hour to which he was limited by his other engagements for his visit here, and he at the same time assured them of the deep respect and gratitude with which he received their numerous manifestations of courtesy and kindness.

The procession again moved on, with four or five elegant volunteer companies escorting, with additional carriages constantly joining the already extended line, with cheers rending the air, handkerchiefs and flags waving from the houses, and bouquets showering upon the President in most fragrant abundance. He paused to kiss a little child who had crowned him with a lovely wreath of flowers, and to exchange salutations with the Rev. Dr. Cox, but he was soon approaching the navy yard, where he passed rapidly through the files of marines at the gate, gave a passing glance at the workshops and improvements around him, shook hands with Captain McKeever and his officers, and with a parting salute from the naval guns, was off again for the ferry. The expedition was a very rapid one, but glorious with excitement and full of pleasure.

At half past two o'clock, with a suitable escort, the Mayor, some of the Committee, and other invited guests, eleven carriages in all, the President started for the "high bridge," and other places of interest on the line of his route. He was first taken to the Distributing Reservoir on forty second Street, and from this part of the great aqueduct, he was furnished, *in memoria rei*, with a cup of pure cold water. Hence, in a few minutes, he was at the Deaf and Dumb Asylum, where the pupils were ready to receive him, and to illustrate before him, the marvellous facility with which the deaf can hear and the dumb can speak. One of the boys welcomed the President, as a bird escaped from his cage, and one of the little girls regretted (and the regret was every where general) that he had not brought Mrs Polk with him. Leaving this beautiful and most touching exhibition, after making his thanks to Mr Peel, the accomplished superintendent of the institution, the President was off again for new sights and fresh objects of interest.

He was soon driven to "Nowlan's," where the company were to take refreshments, and prepare for a further drive. Here numerous introductions took place and a capital dinner was dispatched; and, after a few minutes' delay by a shower which seemed kindly sent on purpose to lay the dust and cool the air, the party was on its way to the bridge. At the Orphan House, about a hundred children were waiting to salute him, and he paused there long enough to address to them a few words of encouragement, and to thank their tutor for his attention.

Soon on his way again, he passed under a beautiful green arch near "McComb's Dam," and about half after six o'clock, alighted at the "High Bridge." This imposing structure, over which is destined to flow nature's own beverage for the half a million of people inhabiting New York, bids fair to excel, when it shall have been completed, any work of the kind in America. Its vast masses of granite, resting upon arches as beautifully turned as they are lofty, strike the beholder with admiration and wonder at the power of human labor when directed by enlightened genius. Man, whose appointed term of life is three score years and ten, is yet enabled to build monuments, which shall bear his name to distant generations, and benefit the world for centuries. Mr Coffin, President of the Board of Water Commissioners, was present at the Bridge, and pointed out all the peculiar points of interest which were connected with its construction. Having thus seen it under the most favorable circumstances, and having given to it all the time he could spare, the President took his leave, and proceeded to the Asylum for the Blind, on Ninth Street.

Here he was received by a large crowd and continued cheers; but making his way through the throng, he was taken in charge by Mr Chamberlain, the Superintendent, who conducted him to the chapel, the band of blind performers playing "Hail Columbia!" as he passed along. In the chapel, which was well filled, also, with spectators were collected the pupils of the Asylum, and numerous fancy articles of their manufacture. Mr Chamberlain lost no time in presenting the President to the unfortunates who were committed to his care, and the President replied with deep feeling, expressing the gratification which his visit gave him, and the additional interest he felt in the institution, for having last season formed an acquaintance with some of its pupils at Washington. Its object, he said, was a noble one, and enlisted the warmest sympathy of every patriot, philanthropist and christian, and its success was full of consolation to its founders and its supporters, as well as to its pupils themselves, who were here taught almost to forget their deprivation, in the happy employments which were found them by their teachers. It indicates with what perfection the mind can be cultivated through the sense of hearing, that a young girl among the pupils, Miss Crosby, recited before the president, the following verses, of her own composing, and recited them, too, with a modesty and appropriateness which would hardly have been increased, had the fair poetess possessed the brightest eyes.

A WELCOME FOR THE PRESIDENT OF THE U.S.

We welcome not a monarch,
    With a crown upon his brow;
Before no haughty sceptre,
    As suppliants we bow.

No gorgeous throne, no princely pomp,
    In this fair land we see;
We boast a true Republic here,
    The home of Liberty.

Oh, be our freedom sacred,
    For dearly was it bought;
To gain the priceless Jewel,
    Our fathers nobly fought.

Tis ours to keep unsullied
    That gem without a stain,
To crush all party spirit,
    Where principle should reign.

We welcome not a monarch,
    But we warmly grasp thy hand,
Our nation's worthy President,
    The guardian of our land.

The Muse of Song hath swept the Lyre,
    Long life and health to thee;
We hail thy mild, benignant ray,
    Thou Star of Tennessee!

We from our constellation miss,
    The Star that once was bright;
That orb has set forever,
    Has faded from our Sight.

The name of Andrew Jackson,
    Will ne'er forgotten be;
The lov'd, the lost, thy kindred Star,
    That rose on Tennessee.

The North, the South, the East, the West,
    Thy name responsive sing;
And the eagle, harmless as the dove,
    Around thee folds its wing.

Thy multifarious duties,
    Forget them for a while,
Nor let a cloud or anxious thought,
    Blend with thy happy Smile.

Pure founts of Joy are gushing,
    In friendship's hallow'd bowers,
And the balmy Zephyrs woo thee,
    To cull the blushing flowers.

Hark, one united burst of Joy,
    By heart and tongue is woke;
One chorus rends the list'ning air,
    Hurrah, for James K. Polk!

Many of the images in these simple lines (interesting only from their origin) are taken from objects of sight; and it is curious to imagine in what forms familiar objects present themselves, to the mental vision of a child born blind. An exquisite touch, it is said, can detect the beauty of a face or the sweetness of a smile, and the blind soon learn to be at home among the flowers. But a star, or a cloud, the sun or the moon, when the blind speak of these, they can have no idea of the actual appearance of the objects of which they speak, however accurately they may have been taught to describe them.

But we were too much in haste at the asylum, to indulge in any such reflections as this; nor could we remain there long enough to pay our respects to a bountiful entertainment which had been provided for the Presidential Party in the dining hall of the establishment. As soon as a passage could be made for us through the crowd, we regained our respective carriages, and soon found ourselves once more in the city. We came down the ninth avenue to Hudson street, down Hudson to Chambers, up Chambers to Broadway and down Broadway to the Astor House, where the President was left by the Mayor in charge of his Democratic friends. A committee was in waiting for him, and without time for supper, he was conducted across the Park, to the old Wigwam of New York Democracy, Tammany Hall. The reception room, on this occasion, was thronged with waiting citizens, as numerous, tho' more orderly, as when in 1844 they made the venerable hall echo and reecho their victorious shouts for "Polk and Dallas." On each side of the room were thirteen banners with the arms and names of the original thirteen states printed thereon in gold characters, each supported by a man in regalia, and at the head of the room was a larger banner bearing this inscription:

Tammany Society

Washington
The father of his Country
or
Columbian Order

On this flag was the figure of a North American Eagle, with its wings extended, and the standard was surmounted by an old fashioned liberty cap.

When the President entered the hall, accompanied by Alderman Purdy, he was placed on the platform directly in front of the Society's banner, where he was introduced by Mr Purdy to the assembled multitude. Six cheers followed, Tammany cheers, and then the President responded:

I am extremely happy, fellow citizens, to meet you here tonight, in Tammany Hall. You are aware that I am making a visit of respect to the Northern States of the Union, and I need not say that I am highly gratified with the reception which I have every where met with; but if it has been more gratifying in one place than another, it has been in the empire City of the empire State. The magnitude of your City, the extent of your population, your institutions, your enterprise, and your rapid growth, are all calculated to impress the observer with feelings of the deepest interest and admiration, and the only regret which I have experienced in witnessing them now, is the regret that I am able to devote to them so little time.

I have endeavored, however, fully to improve the limited opportunity which has been afforded me today; and I appear before you this evening so much fatigued with the exertions which I have made, that I feel wholly unable to address you as I could wish. I trust, therefore, that after cordially renewing to you my thanks for the kindness with which you have this evening welcomed me, and which I beg to assure you, I heartily appreciate, you will permit me to retire to my lodgings, for repose and rest, without detaining you with any further remarks. Fellow citizens, I thank you most sincerely for the warm reception which you have given me, and respectfully bid you, farewell.

The President, then, having taken a seat for a moment, Captain Rynders, President of the Empire Club, said:

Fellow Citizens: I propose that we give three real old fashioned cheers for the President of the United States, such cheers as are heard in Tammany Hall and no where else, and such cheers as only Democrats can give.

The cheers came, long and loud, and then Alderman Purdy appealed to the crowd for a passage out. "Gentlemen," he said, "If there is any place on God's earth where I can take liberties, that place is Tammany Hall. Will you excuse the President from speaking any more, and open a passage for him to go to his hotel and take some rest?" A passage was immediately made for him, and leaning upon the arm of Alderman Purdy, he then left the hall, amid great cheering. A beautiful Serenade, from a German band, closed the day, and it was near midnight before we retired to our chambers, and sought repose.

Sunday June 27

[Rest New York City]

The next day was the Sabbath, and it opened with a morning full of brightness and of beauty, but with an atmosphere, at the same time, of intense heat. The President attended church three times, in the morning, with the Mayor, at St Bartholomew's, where he heard a sermon by Dr. Balch, from the sixth chapter of Romans and twenty fifth verse; in the afternoon, with the Hon. B. F. Butler, to hear Dr Skinner, who preached from the one hundred and thirty-seventh psalm; and in the evening, with Alderman Oliver, at the Dutch Reformed Church, where Dr Scott preached from the ninth of St. Mark and fourth verse.

Between the afternoon and evening services, he found time to make a brief visit with a part of his suite, to the family of Hon. Cornelius Lawrence, with whom he dined, but at his rooms, he avoided, as far as possible, the reception of any visitors. The churches which he attended, were selected for him, not on account of their elegance or their preachers, but because they were attended by those gentlemen whose invitations it seemed proper he should accept. He doubtless heard good sermons and sweet music, and was seated in structures both comfortable and costly; yet I wished he could have seen "Trinity" and "Grace," and have heard, at least, Mr Southard. Trinity is the grandest place of worship in America, and Grace, I am inclined to think, most brilliant. The latter, indeed, on account of the showiness of its interior, has been called the "Opera House."

The President was joined today by Mr Buchanan, Secretary of State, who came from Philadelphia, accompanied by Governor Mouton, of Louisiana, Colonel Mann, of Pennsylvania, and Captain Stein, of the Army, and was to pursue the remainder of the President's journey in his company. The accession was a pleasant and welcome one, and we, all of us, retired for the night, in good spirits and with the brightest hopes.

In New York, the President was invited every where, and was waited on by innumerable committees from other cities and towns. Albany, Rochester, Springfield, Hartford, New Haven, Boston, Charlestown, Lynn, and various other places, were in waiting, by their respective delegates, in the Empire City, and in the most cordial manner solicited his presence among their citizens. Ex President Van Buren, it should be especially noticed, sent him a very courteous and pressing request to pay a visit at Kinderhook, and the towns along the Hudson were extremely urgent that he should pass up that river on his way to Boston. But it was determined to take the route by New Haven and Hartford, and arrangements were made, and answers given accordingly.

Monday June 28

[Departure New York City]

At six o'clock this morning, we took leave of the Astor House, and under escort of Col. Warner's regiment, with a corps of pikemen to clear the way, we were accompanied by a large number of our New York friends, to the slip where we were to take the Steamer for New Haven. Of course, a large crowd was there before us, but we had no difficulty in getting a passage through it, and were soon on board the "Hero," listening to the cheers and the reports of cannon, which marked the occasion of the President's departure. We had with us now, Ex Governor Mouton, Commodore Stewart, Col Mann and Capt. Stein, besides Mr Buchanan and the gentlemen who started with the President from Washington.

Committees were with us, also, from New Haven, Hartford and Boston, and as far as the former place we were accompanied by Alderman Purser, and Assistant Alderman Kohler, of New York. In addition to these gentlemen, too, we had of course a large number on board, who were present merely from curiosity or to show their good-will to the occasion. The company being thus arranged and ready for the trip, the signal of departure was given by the usual ringing of the bell. Three cheers followed for the President: the band we had with us struck up "Hail, Columbia!" a salute was fired nearby, and we were off from New York, and *en route* for New England.

Again we were saluted from the guns of the Navy Yard, and as we moved along, new cheers awaited us, but we made rapid progress and speedily left behind all traces of the mighty city in whose midst we had just witnessed so much animation, business and life. Where Henry Hudson, in the "Crescent," on his return to Europe, in 1609 could look back only upon majestic forests and savage villages, we left a magnificent metropolis, swarming with population, abounding in the arts and ornaments of civilization, and constantly advancing in prosperity and ferver, by the force of its unlimited enterprise and the favor of its admirable position. Who can estimate its wealth and its greatness, as they will be exhibited a century hence; when it may have large cities for suburbs, and will count its inhabitants by millions. By means of the improved facilities of communication in modern times, there is scarcely any limit to be placed to the growth of cities, and even an unfortunate creation redeems itself from neglect by the enterprise which unites it to more fertile regions.

New York, however, has the social faults which belong to an eminently business place, and to a shifting, moneymaking people. Everything there is confused, and every man there is busily pursuing some selfish aim. One who walks slowly in the streets is in danger of being run over, and every body is so much in a hurry there that, in such a case, no resident would probably stop to pick him up. To this general character of the city, there are of course exceptions, particularly among the old Knickerbockers. But these last compose now but a very small part of the population of the city. It is a place where men congregate from all directions, not for the purpose of comfortable living or social enjoyment, but for the single and undisguised object of making money. It has little of the stable, mature appearance which belong to the home of ancient families. But, on the other hand, it has none of the moss and sluggishness of antiquity; and repose and luxury, after all, are very sure to come to it in good time. Let us leave it with thankfulness for its really liberal hospitality, and with our cordial wishes for its future welfare.

We had an excellent breakfast on board the "Hero," and a beautiful excursion to New Haven. Messrs Wilcox, Blackman, and Bristol were the committee from that place, and their mission was well performed. We reached their lovely city of Elms at about eleven o'clock. The Mayor and appropriate escorts were in readiness at the landing, and a national salute announced the arrival of the President. He was, then, received into an elegant barouche, and all the members of his party having also been distributed in carriages, was taken in procession around the city, the military leading the way and a cavalcade of citizens bringing up the rear on horseback, all the while sonorous music blowing martial sounds. At the very commencement of our route, we passed under an arch extending across the street, on which in large letters, was blazoned the inscription

"Welcome to New England"

As we moved on, flags and banners were displayed, bouquets were showered upon the President's barouche, bright eyes were radiant at the windows, and every thing wore the pleasing aspect of hospitality and kindness. In front of one of the dwellings which we passed, I observed the engraved portrait of the President, encircled by a wreath of flowers, while from the windows and balcony of the same dwelling, the waving of handkerchiefs, denoted the hearty warmth with which its occupants greeted the city's guest. Having visited the principal streets, the procession was conducted to the beautiful public square of the place; and here we left our carriages and entered the City Hall.

In the Hall the President was introduced to the City Councils, and to many distinguished citizens; and, afterwards, he attempted to shake hands with all the crowd from without, who poured in at one door and went out at the opposite front. But this was found to be too much of a task, for the rush was almost suffocating; the hand-shaking, therefore, was dispensed with, and the people were obliged to content themselves with *seeing* the President. To this rule, the ladies of course were exceptions, and their hands, on such an occasion, were not refused. When the pressure of the multitude had a little subsided, the teachers and pupils of the New Haven Schools came in, and presented one of the most interesting features of the whole day. The President then rested himself, with his friends, in one of the less public rooms of the building,

but in a few minutes placed himself at the disposal of the officers
of Yale College for a visit to their institution and students.

We were taken first to the College Chapel, where we listened
to a national hymn and chorus from the Beethoven Society. And
then, passing on our way through two lines of students, who gave
the President three hearty cheers, we went to the library, to
the Trumbull Gallery, and to the Cabinet of Curiosities belong-
ing to the institution. In the library, a new and elegant building
finished in its interior, in gothic style, were several of the older
officers who had had connection with the College, and one of the
gentlemen present was introduced as a patriarch of the revolution.
The reputation of Col. Trumbull, an alumnus of Yale, is national,
for he attested his patriotism both by his sword and his pencil.
Four of his historical paintings adorn the rotunda of the Capitol
at Washington. But it was not without interest that we examined
his minor productions in this gallery of his native State. Some
of them seemed to have little intrinsic merit, but they deserve to
be perpetuated, for the sake of their antiquity and their author.
In the Cabinet, we were all struck with a lock of hair from the
head of Major André, and with an original pen & ink sketch of
himself from his own hand. Copies of this sketch have been multiplied, and he is generally known by our countrymen as having
been a young man of fine appearance as well as great misfortune.
From the Library we were escorted to the "Tontine" for dinner.
And again, upon leaving the college grounds, the President was
greeted with hearty and enthusiastic cheers from the assembled
students.

Yale College is surrounded with many interesting associations, for with the single exception of "Harvard," it is the most
ancient college in America. Its history dates as far back as
1700, and during the revolution, many of its students suspended
study and assumed arms. A striking class, about that period,
is mentioned as having contained, among other noted characters,
Noah Webster, Joel Barlow, Oliver Wolcott Jr, and Uriah Tracy.
Singularly enough. The President had visited New Haven in
the year 1834, and had then placed four young gentlemen from
Tennessee, in charge of the Officers of "Yale." Of these, one
was his brother, two were his nephews, and one the son of a

friend; and one of the nephews, J. Knox Walker, is now his private secretary, having graduated in 1838. The college, therefore, in extending its hospitalities to the President, only repaid the honor which it had received from Mr Polk, in its selection by that gentleman as the place of education for his nearest relatives and friends. And this consideration, among some of its officers at least, was not, I am inclined to think, wholly forgotten, on the occasion of our visit now.

We awaited dinner at the hotel for upwards of half an hour, which, with our limited time, was equivalent to losing it altogether. In point of fact, we had hardly seated ourselves at the table, the Mayor presiding, and a goodly number of guests keeping us company, when the time was come for our departure by the special train for Hartford. This was a misfortune, certainly, but we were pledged to pass the night at Springfield, and to delay longer at New Haven was only to reduce unreasonably the time we had allotted to Hartford. The President, therefore, after we had despatched a *very* "hasty plate of soup," was compelled to explain to his friends the necessity for then leaving them. And after the Mayor had proposed his health (which was drunk with three cheers) we retired from the dining hall, and were soon on our way in carriages to the Hartford depot. We were suitably escorted thither, but being a little behind the time, the train only waited for us to be comfortably seated in the car provided, before it moved off at its most rapid rate, towards the city of the Charter Oak.

We had passed the time in New Haven very pleasantly, and unanimously voted it one of the most delightful places in the Union. It has every where an appearance of Yankee thrift, and nothing can exceed the elegant comfort of its dwellings or the beauty of its numerous trees. We found its citizens, also, full of kindness, and although we were obliged to leave the dinner which had been prepared for us, untasted, or rather unfinished, yet we saw enough of it, to satisfy us of its value, and to make us regret most heartily the necessity which prevented us from doing full justice to it. We had with us from New Haven to Hartford, Governor Toucey, Judge Niles, Hon. Jas. Dixon, and several other gentlemen of those places. We left the cars just in the outskirts of Hartford, where we found carriages, and a handsome mounted cavalcade in readiness to receive us. In this way, we found the approach to the city very beautiful, and had an opportunity of passing through the pleasant grounds of the Asylum for the Insane. In front of this institution were seen some of its officers and inmates, and the President's carriage paused long enough to enable one of the latter, a young and interesting girl, to present to him a superb bouquet.

We then moved on, admiring the cultivated country through which we went, until we reached the borders of the city proper. Here several military companies were added to our escort, and our way was made through crowded streets, under waving banners and handkerchiefs, and amid the sound of music and the ringing of bells. We passed by lines of school-children, who received us with cheers, and saw very many delicious residences, whose occupants we almost envied. Among the latter, was the pretty cottage of Mrs Sigourney, the poetess, at whose gate the procession halted, while she herself appeared on her balcony to greet the President as he passed. She improved the opportunity to send us all a glass of cool water, which, after a long and dusty ride, we found as refreshing as a spring in the desert to a thirsty traveler. We regretted to learn afterwards, that this pause was taken advantage of for a very different purpose. A thief employed it as a convenient season for robbing the accomplished lady of a gold watch and several articles of jewelry which he removed from a table in her *boudoir*. It was with real satisfaction, that we were informed in Lowell, that the property had been recovered and the thief committed for trial. We had a long ride about Hartford, under a scorching sun, and were really glad, although the place is a beautiful one, to leave our carriages for a little rest and refreshment at the City Hotel. A nice collation was here provided, after which we were taken to the cars for Springfield, Governor Toucey, by invitation of the President, bearing us company to that town, and thence, also to Boston, Lowell, and Concord. Very strangely, he had been to neither of these places before, although an old resident of Hartford and one of its most distinguished citizens.

We reached Springfield late in the evening, were received

with the ringing of bells, and the firing of guns, and taken without delay to our lodgings at Warrener's Hotel. Here we had every thing in admirable order, and found an elegant supper awaiting us, at which the Hon. Mr Ashmun, Major Ripley, and various other distinguished gentlemen assisted. Here were many ladies and gentlemen, also, in the parlors and drawingrooms of the house, who had an opportunity to see the President for a few minutes, after supper; but he soon retired, and all the members of his party were glad to follow his example. We had earned a good night's rest by a fatiguing day's work. We had breakfasted in New York, dined in Connecticut, and supped in Massachusetts.

Tuesday June 29

[Reception Boston]

It rained a little during the night, but from the promise of the morning, we anticipated a pleasant day for our ride to Boston. Colonels Bigelow and Rotch, Aids to Governor Briggs, met the President at Springfield, and we had with us, also the Boston Committee, consisting of Aldermen Parker and Head, and Councilmen Whiting, Seaver and Bailey, while Marshal Isaac O. Barnes, and Navy Agent Joseph Nall, kept us company on the way from pure good will. The Boston Committee had been with us, in whole or part, ever since we left New York, and we were deeply indebted to Messrs. Parker and Whiting especially, for numerous attentions and civilities which were always rendered in the kindest and most cordial manner. Under such auspices, after a good breakfast at "Warrener's" (which, by the way, is one of the most elegant hotels in the country) we took leave of Springfield at eight o'clock A.M. in a special train of cars. It was a pity we were obliged to pass through this town so hastily. It is on every account well worth seeing. It was first settled in 1635, and then called by its Indian name of "Agawam." In 1786 it was invaded by the celebrated "Shays," during the rebellion of that name, and its Court House seized upon. It suffered very much also in the early Indian wars. It is beautifully situated on the east side of

Connecticut River, and numbers a population of about twenty thousand. It makes the point of meeting for the Hartford, the Albany, the Northampton and the Boston railroads, and having a fine soil and an abundance of water power, cannot fail to become at an early day, a place of great importance. The U.S. Armory is in Springfield, under the superintendence of Major Ripley, who went with us to the tri-mountain city. We were distant from it ninety eight miles, but our iron horse was sure to have us there in four hours, and we were out of the depot almost before the multitude assembled there could finish their parting cheers.

Along we went through pleasant villages and over a smiling country, the President cheered at every succeeding settlement, until at about ten o'clock we approached Worcester. It had now become cloudy, and when we reached the depot in that town, the rain poured down in torrents. Nevertheless, the President was introduced at the end of the car to a great many people, and in spite of the weather, we were soon off again for Boston. We had no time to pause in Roxbury, though its Mayor, Genl Dearborn, had pressingly invited us to do so, and we reached the mill dam in Boston at precisely twelve o'clock. Our coming had been announced by a salute of heavy guns, and on the causeway we were met by the city authorities, were received by a military escort of Light Infantry and Lancers, under Colonel Edmunds, and without loss of time, were conducted to the City proper.

It rained almost all the time, but the order of procession was yet carried out with great fidelity. The military, the Engine companies, the Schools, the various associations, the marshals, almost all kept constant to their places, and a very large number of people braved the storm in the streets. The banners, the flags of welcome, the handkerchiefs, and the crowded windows, as well as the heartiness of occasional cheers, indicated how brilliant could have been the reception, had the Bostonians been favored with a clear day. But they were not responsible for the weather, any more than they were for the article in the Boston Advertiser, advising them not to receive the President with public honors, and they accomplished on the occasion, every thing that could possibly have been expected of them. Our lodgings were at the Revere House, and after a ride of upwards of two hours through the streets, we reached our destination at three o'clock. We found here Governor Briggs, ex Governors Mouton, Fairfield, Anderson, Woodbury, and various committees of welcome from other places in the neighborhood, and farther east; and the President was at once received by Gov. Briggs, in behalf of the authorities of the Commonwealth. The Governor addressed him as follows.

Mr President. In the name of the citizens of Massachusetts, I tender to you as Chief Magistrate of the United States, their respects, and bid you welcome to the hospitalities of the Commonwealth. I should be happy, Sir, if your official duties would allow you the time, to go with you throughout our State, and show you our people and their institutions as they are. I should be pleased to have you go, among our farmers upon the mountains, and in the vallies and upon the distant cape, that you might see the difficulties they have had to encounter in cultivating a hard, unyielding soil, when that soil is compared in fertility and productiveness with the rich bottom lands and wide prairies of your own great West. To go into the shops of our mechanics, the factories of our manufactures, the stores of our merchants, and the marts of commerce; upon the docks of our Seaports, and upon the decks of our merchant vessels and our well-equipped Whale Ships. To show you our colleges, academies, and seminaries of learning, and to go into our district schools, the cherished objects of the people of the Commonwealth from their earliest settlement, and to visit with you the temples of religion erected in every village and neighborhood.

I know, Sir, you would be pleased to witness the varied and persevering industry of our people. But, Sir, while the citizens of Massachusetts are engaged with untiring perseverance in those avocations by which they hope to promote their prosperity and happiness, they remember that they belong to that great family of states over which you have been called to preside by the suffrages of a free people. To this union, our people, individually and as a state, acknowledge their obligations and they intend faithfully and always to fulfil those obligations. That Union, under a general government, conducted according to the provisions of the glorious constitution established by the wise patriots of a past generation, steadily progressing in the principles of liberty, civilization and christianity, they trust in Heaven will be perpetual. We shall ever rejoice to see your administration contribute to that important end.

The President replied in substantially the following words.

Sir. In receiving from you, the Chief Magistrate of the ancient Commonwealth, the welcome with which you have now honored me, I am sensible that your purpose is not merely a personal one, but that you seek rather to recognize a great principle of our government. I feel that it is the office which I hold that you wish to honor; and while you thus honor it through me, I do not forget that I am but the humble representative of the people, for the time being, owing to them this expression of your respect, and responsible to them for all my public acts. I hear with deep satisfaction of the advancing prosperity of your State, and should be most happy to extend my visit, within its borders, to all those interesting features of its condition to which you have alluded; to see its free schools, its academies, and its higher seminaries of learning; to observe its workshops and its manufactures; to go among your agricultural districts and witness there the rewarded labors of your industrious husbandmen.

I should thus, no doubt, be able to strengthen my impressions of the resources of your Commonwealth, and the energy and enterprise and virtue of your inhabitants, and to rejoice, as I most assuredly should, in the growth and prosperity of one of the foremost states of the old thirteen, which composed our original Union. But pleasant and profitable as would be this employment, it would be incompatible with my public duties. In a few days I must return to the Seat of Government. Your allusion to the Union meets my hearty response. There is an altar at which we may all worship. However much we may differ about local or temporary questions of policy, on the question of the Union, we are all united. We recognize the Union in every one of our public acts. We recognize it now and here. In the imposing welcome which you have now extended to me, I see but the fact that the whole Union is receiving honor, through its representative, from one of the States which form the Union. For the respectful manner in which this honor has been accorded to me, I return you, Sir, my most cordial thanks.

The President then received his friends, including the officers who had been on duty during the day, the officers of the Army and Navy, and numerous citizens and strangers of distinction. There were ten or twelve of the gentlemen present, including Governor Briggs, who had served with the President in Congress, and who could greet him, therefore, with something more than official courtesy. After receiving company for about two hours, he retired to rest and to prepare for dinner. His private apartments were as rich and elegant as good taste and lavish expenditure could well make them. In the beauty of their appointments they far exceeded any rooms which he had occupied since leaving Washington. The house and furniture were both new, and his own apartments had been decorated, in addition, especially for him.

When the President reached the borders of Boston and was met by the city authorities, as has been already stated, he was addressed by Hon. Josiah Quincy Jr, Mayor of the City, in an official welcome which we were unable to hear, but which was reported in the newspapers as follows.

Mr. President. In behalf of the citizens of Boston I welcome the Chief Magistrate of the Union to the Metropolis of Massachusetts. I welcome you as officially the representative of those, whose fathers stood by ours in the days of the revolution, and of the twenty millions who now, with us, constitute this great confederacy. I welcome you, as a Statesman, to an acquaintance with the men, and to an examination of the institutions of New England. To an acquaintance with men whose industry, intelligence and enterprise have clothed this barren soil with plenty, and made it the abode of art and science, of virtue and religion. To an examination of the institutions, particularly of the free school, the peculiar institution of our land, by which, with the blessing of Heaven, we hope to continue a race of intelligent freemen, who will understand, maintain and transmit the liberties and virtues of their fathers to the end of time. We receive you, as we received your predecessors in office, and ask that you will grant us as they did, the honor of considering you the guest of the city during your stay among us.

The President responded, it is said, substantially as follows.

Mr. Mayor. For this manifestation of respect from the citizens of Boston, I beg you to receive my most sincere thanks. Most happy should I be, if my limited time would permit, to visit the institutions of which you have spoken. I am fully aware of the benevolent purpose which your ancient Commonwealth has always kept in view, in maintaining a general system of education. Under our form of Government, the education of the people is of the highest importance; for upon their intelligence must depend the perpetuity of that Government. I am gratified to hear of the success with which you have provided for this great result; and shall be pleased, so far as I can, to witness the prosperity which has crowned your efforts, in whatever has for its object the improvement of the people or the honor of our common country. Again, Sir, I thank you for this hospitable welcome to your honored city.

After these addresses and while the procession moved through Beacon Street, Hon Harrison Gray Otis appeared upon the balcony of his house and courteously exchanged salutations with the President. Hon. Abbot Lawrence, also, manifested a similar spirit of courtesy as the procession passed the elegant mansion occupied by him.

At 7 o'clock came the official dinner, in the spacious hall of the Revere House, which was handsomely decorated for the occasion. The mayor presided, and a very large number of guests did ample justice to the rich viands with which Mr Stevens had this evening supplied his tables. A fine band of music was in attendance, and to that and their own thoughts and conversation, the company were exclusively indebted for any animation which attended the dinner—for there was no wine. The temperance question had been recently agitated in the city councils, and the mayor had declined presiding at the tables in the presence of wine. It was determined, therefore, to banish wine, and retain the mayor.

Each of us, however, was provided with a plentiful supply of liquors in our private apartments. I know not which was in worse taste—the frigid temperance of the dining hall, or the bar-room supply of the sleeping chambers. Both, doubtless, were well meant; but in the one case it seems to me, there was a needless sacrifice to bigotry, and in the other, an equally needless offering to hypocrisy. The dinner, which [was] very elegant, occupied us an hour and a half, and the mayor, after a few remarks upon the *etiquette* which, on so distinguished an occasion, dispensed with sentiments and bumpers, informed the company that the President, in order to meet another engagement, was obliged then to withdraw. They were followed at once from the hall by nearly all the guests, who seemed to be unanimously of opinion that a cold-water dinner was not entitled to more than an hour and a half's attention.

The remainder of the evening was devoted by the President to the further reception of company, and notwithstanding the inclemency of the evening, a large number of citizens improved the opportunity to see and take him by the hand.

On the whole, Boston acquitted itself very handsomely in its reception of the President, and whatever else may be said of it it is a snug retreat in a rainy day. But let us do it entire Justice, and with a full conviction of its weaknesses, and faults, we must admit at last that it deserves no stinted praise. It is excessive in its admiration of itself, but it has really much in it which is worthy of admiration. It is greedy after wealth, but then it spends it like a prince. It is a little puritan in its notions, but puritanism is better than its reverse, and after all, wine may be had, even in Boston, if it is drunk in secret. It clamors against war, but it supplies good soldiers. It has sometimes given birth to moral treason; but it has always contained a pure leaven of uncorruptible patriotism. It was the birthplace of Franklin. It was the home of Hancock. It contains the cradle of American liberty.

Its history goes back to the clearest fountains of our country's origin. And what has it worked out for itself. Its population is not less than 115,000, of which a hundred thousand has been the growth of the last half century. Its wealth has increased more rapidly than its population. Its religious institutions may be understood, when it is considered that it has eighty churches, which cost about three millions and a half and can accommodate about ninety thousand persons. For education, it expends on its schools 206,000 dollars, exclusive of the cost of private instruction, every year. Its charities are its noblest feature, and in this respect there is no city in America to be compared with it. In a single year (1845) it gave away, for various purposes of beneficence, upwards of three hundred thousand dollars, and its charities for the last twenty years, are estimated in a recent calculation, at ten millions. In this way she surely adorns the confederacy, while, in spite of her Abolition mania, she promotes the Union of the States, by the enterprize and wealth with she helps to bind them together by railroads and canals. A single firm of mercantile men in Boston have just bought the Roanoke railroad in Virginia.

Let us remember, then, its greatness, and we shall almost forget its meanness. Many faults may be pardoned to a city of so many virtues. It was the seat of the anti-revolutionary "tea party," of the rencontre with the British troops, known as the "Boston Massacre," was so hostile to England and rebellious, that its charter was once taken away and its port shut up, and was the first place besieged by Great Britain after the revolution began. It is situated on a small peninsula, but needing more land, it has 'made' it by damming out the water. A large number of its principal streets are on 'made land.' It is in full view of Bunkers Hill, and near neighbor to Charlestown, where the President was to be received the following day.

Wednesday June 30

[Tour Boston, Charlestown, and Lowell]

We had a fair day for Charlestown, and for Lowell. At 8 o'clock A.M. the President went with Mayor Quincy to see Faneuil Hall, and Quincy Market, and on his return received the visits of his friends. About ten o'clock, with a large attendance of distinguished persons, and under escort of the "Independent Cadets," who marched to splendid music, he started for Charlestown. A sub-committee of the Charlestown Council—Messrs. Willard and Moore—were with him. On the Warren bridge he was met by Geo. W. Warren, Mayor of Charlestown, at the head of a new escort, and passed into his barouche. He was then preceded by a long cavalcade, followed by a train of carriages, and by members of the fire department, and accompanied by an escort of military companies, towards Monument Square. The whole procession was under the direction of Edward Riddle, Chief Marshal. As it crossed the bridge, salutes were fired from the Navy Yard, and from the Revenue Cutter Hamilton; and another salute was fired when it reached the square. Bunker Hill presented a beautiful scene. The monument was gaily decorated with lines of flags and banners and pennants, extending from its summit to its base, and running off at each corner in an angle of fifty degrees, to the ground. On the north side of the square, a platform had been raised, upon which was erected a pavilion, splendidly ornamented with flags and bunting and wreaths of flowers, and the floor of which was carpeted and furnished with chairs. Upon this platform was the President, with Governor Briggs, the Mayors of Boston and Charlestown, and other distinguished persons. A place upon one side of the Square was reserved for the children of the public schools, and about two thousand of them were present, while within the Square there were four or five thousand spectators besides.

The President was transferred to the charge of Mayor Warren in a few brief remarks, and the latter then welcomed him to Charlestown in the following words.

Mr President. The city of Charlestown is glad publicly to receive upon her most favored spot, the President of the United States. Seventy two years ago, Mr President, it was decided on this very ground that the land which our Pilgrim fathers sought to reclaim from the wilderness, should be a free heritage to their descendants, who would e'er long become a mighty and prosperous nation. At the time of the revolutionary conflict, that distant state of your adoption, which has had the honor to give two Presidents to our beloved Union, was not then known by name, even as a colony. But Tennessee now takes a stand amongst the most important States of the Confederacy. For American civilization and enterprise, advancing with the spirit of liberty, and forming new states in their progress, have now transcended as far beyond her borders, as she is removed by distance from Massachusetts Bay. Fortunate, fortunate, Sir, is your lot to have been called by the suffrages of the people to preside over this great republic. During your administration has an important treaty been negotiated with that ambitious and powerful nation of the old world, whose policy it was to repress the tide of American population and republican institutions from extending on the shores of the Pacific. The concession made to the United States in the Oregon Treaty, and the unexampled condition of the commercial and political relations which they now sustain to Great Britain, present *our* Country, as she now is, in striking contrast with the position of the thirteen colonies, at the time when his majesty, George IIId offered a public reward for the apprehension of "two notorious rebels," John Hancock and Samuel Adams. Impartial history has rescued those immortal names from that opprobrious imputation, and has placed them high in the ranks of the heroes and the patriots of the nation. So will it ever be—that posterity will do ample justice to great men and noble deeds.

May your Administration, Mr President, be also, successful, in accomplishing the desire which you have so frequently expressed, of establishing a permanent treaty of peace with our sister republic. And when, by the favor of Providence, in the fulness of time, such a treaty shall be effected, may all the arts of peace and of a refined civilization be assiduously cultivated in every portion of this favored country. May her industrial energies, her sagacious enterprise, and her virtue and intelligence continue to mark her rapid advancement. May her lengthening bands of iron, which unite her states in friendly communication, be multiplied. May those electric sparks of intelligence fly with the rapidity of lightning, from the Atlantic across to the Pacific, from the North to the South, animating by one instantaneous touch, the whole American heart with one feeling of harmonious concord.

Here, as every where else, was hailed with approbation, the announcement formally made by you, Mr President, upon entering on the duties of your August Office, that, though you were elected to it by a party, it would be your aim to be the President, not of a party, but of the whole country. May that magnanimous sentiment which has recently been reiterated by you, ever actuate the conduct of those who shall hereafter succeed you in this most exalted of all earthly stations. The official visits of the Chief Magistrate of our republic to its remotest sections, and the public reception of him will always have a tendency to induce such a course; they will also serve to perpetuate a harmony of social and political feeling, the more necessary to the nation the more populous and powerful it shall become. The people of the United States are Sovereign and independent, accustomed and authorized by the Magna Charta of liberty, to form their own religious and political opinions; while, at the same time, they all alike yield, with a graceful and courteous spirit, to the will of the majority constitutionally expressed. This freedom of thought and action, and this submission to the popular voice, form the solid rock foundation of our national greatness.

In the name of the City of Charlestown, and by the unanimous authority of her government, I bid you a genuine cordial welcome to her precincts. She does not boast of the magnificence and sumptuous splendor which older and richer cities may display, but she offers an open hand and a generous heart. Here dwell the industrious citizens who help to build the ships of our nation, and others who are employed, in the various pursuits of labor and of skill, all of whom, breathing this liberal air and nurtured in the principles of the revolution, are strong in their allegiance, and are ever ready to defend them. She presents to you her public schools, where all her children, upon the broad platform of equality, are so instructed in knowledge and in virtue, that under the benignant smiles of Heaven, they may become worthy sons and daughters of our great republic. In the name of Charlestown, I bid you welcome to Bunker Hill. Its soil entombed with the blood of our forefathers, is the peculiar boast and pride of this city. But its principles are widespread over the land; they are the birthright of every American. This monument, lifting its lofty summit to the skies, stands, and will stand forever, proclaiming these principles to the remotest generation, and in every hour of threatened dissention or danger, invoking, in solemn silence, intelligent millions to be reunited in their defence.

We heartily thank you, Mr President, for coming here to testify your respect and interest in this memorable spot; and when hereafter, Sir, you shall retire from the weary cares of official labor to the tranquil enjoyment of a private station, and shall recall the incidents of your eventful life, may the reminiscences of the present hour be a source of unalloyed gratification. And be assured, Mr President, that the city will remember with pleasure, that, as in former times, so even on this day, she has been honored by a visit from one whom her beloved country has honored, by having placed him at her head.

The President replied to the following effect.

He said there was not to be found throughout our extended country a spot more interesting to the patriot, than that on which he then stood. The welcome which he had received from the City of Charlestown, was doubly gratifying, from having been on Bunker's Hill. Since he had entered upon his present tour, he had visited no place better fitted to awaken emotions of gratitude and admiration for those heroic men who, by suffering and privation and toil and blood, established our country's freedom; for here was made one of the noblest and earliest of that series of revolutionary efforts, by which American liberty was at last secured. The lesson which it taught, was one of duty as well as gratitude, & invoked us, as patriots and as freemen, to preserve with fidelity, our invaluable institutions, and to cherish with unceasing vigilance, that political Union, upon which their existence depends. For what the Mayor had been pleased to say of his services since he had held the office of Chief Magistrate of the United States, he expressed his sincere and hearty thanks. His endeavor, in that responsible station, had always been to do his duty; and while he was fully sensible that he had not been secure against those imperfections of judgement which attend upon all, he yet earnestly hoped that the measures which he had adopted, might not prove to be without fortunate results, and that at the close of his administration, he might leave his country prosperous and happy. Posterity, he hoped, would long enjoy and appreciate the inestimable privileges of our free government. Our system of public schools afforded ground for this hope. If rightly taught, our successors would have intelligence enough to understand the advantages bequeathed to them, and firmness and patriotism enough to protect and defend them.

The President, having concluded his remarks, amid the most hearty cheers, was now conducted into the monument, and around the square, so that the immense crowds of citizens who were on the hill, could have an opportunity to see him; and they greeted him, on every side, with the most generous enthusiasm.   He was then, with his friends, taken to the house of the Mayor, where a handsome collation had been prepared. After the colla- tion, the Mayor of Boston thanked the Mayor and authorities of Charlestown, for their liberal hospitalities to the guest of Boston, who had been received as warmly, he said, as the enemies of our country had been received by their ancestors. The Navy Yard in Charlestown with its admirable Dry Dock, would have well repaid a visit, and its officers expected one, but there was not sufficient time for it, and it was not therefore made. From the house of Mayor Warren, the President, with his friends, was es- corted back to the bridge, and thence re-conducted to the Revere House, where, after another collation, and many adieux, they took carriages for the Lowell depot. The President was loudly cheered as he took his seat in the barouche assigned him, and had a military escort to the cars. The committee from Lowell were Messrs Brown, Whipple, and Fellows, and their arrangements had been well made, and were successfully carried out. We left Boston, amid cheers and shouts from the multitude at the depot, about two o'clock P.M.; and in an hour's time, were halted just at the entrance to Lowell, where a platform had been erected for the ceremonies of the occasion. On this platform the President was welcomed by Jefferson Bancroft Esq, Mayor of the City, to the Manchester of America. He spoke of the rapid growth of Lowell, and of its present great prosperity, and alluded to the fact that twenty five years ago, he was himself an operative in one of its factories. The President replied with great felicity, all the better for speaking in the open air.

He said he had long desired to visit the northern section of his country, and was especially glad of an opportunity to see and examine its manufacturing establishments. We were all interested in the suc- cess of the industrial pursuits of our people, but those who administered

our public affairs, were particularly called upon to study and to examine them. It was with great satisfaction, therefore, that he had
come to the City of Lowell, to witness for himself, the results of its
prosperous devotion to the labors of the loom. These results, of capital
combined with industry, were now matters of history, and he rejoiced
that they were so full of usefulness and encouragement. Associated, as
he was, in the government of the nation, there was no department of
business or of labor, in which he did not feel a deep and constant interest.
Agriculture, commerce manufactures—they were all the handmaids of
each other—and the national prosperity was best accomplished by their
efficient and harmonious cooperation. The growth of Lowell was a striking illustration of our country's progress, but it must have been occa-
sioned, in a great degree, by the sterling qualities of its early population.
Its citizens have reaped the reward of their efforts in their own success,
as well as in the advancing wealth and increasing importance of this city.
Twenty five years ago, Sir, you were yourself an operative, as you have
told us, in yonder factories, and now you preside over a city of thirty
thousand people. Your history is the history of a Franklin. The history
of thousands of those self-made men, who are so closely identified with
our country's interests. It reveals the strength and genius of our government, and accounts for the rapid spread of our institutions and the marvellous growth of our republic. The workingmen of America constitute
its true power and glory. They make up its legitimate sovereignty, and
lie at the foundation of all its success. As one of their responsible ser-
vants, I tender you my cordial thanks for the hospitable welcome which
I have received to your city, and assure you that it will give me sincere
pleasure, to examine your institutions, and so far as I may have it in my
power, to become acquainted with your citizens.

The President concluded his remarks amid repeated and
hearty cheers, and was then received into a barouche, and his
Suite being also provided with carriages, was escorted through
the principal streets of the city. There was a fine turnout, in
the procession, of the Irish Benevolent Society, and a long cavalcade of citizens on horseback, while the display of the factory
girls, or ladies of the mills, as they sometimes call themselves,
was something not soon to be forgotten. There was the usual
number of flags and handkerchiefs waving in the streets, and one
banner attracted attention, with the inscription, "Welcome, the
Chief Magistrate of the Union: Our Country, however bounded."
There was a very general turn-out, too, of the people, and when

the procession reached his lodgings at the Merrimack House, a congregation of some ten thousand persons had assembled in one dense body, in front of the hotel. They had a good opportunity of seeing the President, who appeared for a little time on a platform prepared for the occasion, and their curiosity having been thus gratified, he withdrew to his private apartments.

After the President had rested for half an hour, we were conducted to dinner in Mechanics Hall. There were four tables, bountifully supplied, and about two hundred persons were seated at them. The mayor presided, and Rev. Amos Blanchard invoked the divine blessing, after which every man consulted his palate and the bill of fare. After dinner the President received his friends, and most of his suite went out to see the extensive works which were in progress by the factory-owners for the purpose of increasing their water-power. The evident difficulty and cost of these works, indicated very clearly the value of the power sought and the prosperous condition of those who sought it. We retired early, in expectation of a visit to the factories before breakfast in the morning. After breakfast, we were to go to Concord.

Thursday July 1

[Arrival Concord]

At six o'clock we went under the auspices of Saml Lawrence, Esq, and Mayor Bancroft, to see the interior of the Babel factories. We went into a carpet, a cotton, a cassimere, a calico, printing, establishment, saw any number of machines, both dumb and human, wondered a little at the extensive and costly scale on which every thing was managed, and returned to our hotel, with fine appetites for breakfast. I know not how it is with others, but I never go into a factory, without a feeling of regret that such an establishment should be necessary. So many human beings shut up twelve hours a day, amid so much noise, in so bad an atmosphere, and with such mechanical employment, surely, surely cannot be in the meet fulfilment of the great purposes of their creation. The policy, too, of accumulating in a small space that vast and dependent population, which is the natural growth of a manufacturing town, seems to me to be of very doubtful utility. Not in such places are republican spirits and Spartan hearts best educated. Not there will be increased, the virtue, the happiness, the true glory of the nation. Better, far better, the free air, and vigorous health, and thoughtful leisure, which attend upon the pursuits of Agriculture, and all history enforces the substantial truth of this reflection. "I marvel," says President Humphrey, (and who does not share his wonder) "how so many sensible mothers can consent to part with their daughters, and how the daughters can be willing to come, down from their green, fleece-clad hills, and exchange their bright skies, and healthy breezes and widespread landscapes, for the confinement of heated rooms, the annoyance of chemical odors, and the deafening chatter of a thousand handed machinery."

We breakfasted at Seven O'clock, and at eight were off for Concord, N.H. Senator Atherton, Ex Governor Hill, Postmaster Greene, of Boston, and a full deputation from New Hampshire, were with us on the way, in addition to the augmented *suite* with which we left Boston. At Nashua, we found a large crowd at the depot, who cheered most lustily, and with the true spirit. The President was introduced to them by Mr Atherton, who resides here, and made a few pertinent remarks in reply. Mr Buchanan, Mr Clifford, Com. Stewart, Capt. Stein, and others, were also introduced, and then the train started again, leaving behind as enthusiastic a crowd, as we would wish to see. At Nashua, Adjt. Gen. Oliver and Col. Choate, took leave of the President, on behalf of Massachusetts. At Manchester, there was another uproarious crowd. Judge Upham presented the President to them; the President replied, and then Judge Woodbury addressed them.

Soon we were off once more, pausing as we reached the monument of General Stark, and arriving at Concord about ten o'clock. The military met us at the outer edge of the town; the President and company were placed in barouches, and thus we were escorted through the town, followed by a procession of citizens, on horseback and on foot. Every thing here indicated enthusiasm and joy. The cheers came loud and long, and the ladies were particularly earnest in their displays of welcome. Across the street from Governor Hill's residence, was a beautiful arch, on which was inscribed, "The Ladies of the Granite State Welcome the President to the Capital." After a dusty, but still very gratifying ride, we arrived at the American House (Gass's) and were conducted to our rooms. On the upper gallery of the portico, fronting the main street, the President and the distinguished people with him, were introduced to the people, and were received with tumultuous applause. Next came the proceedings in the State House. At two o'clock the Senate and House met in Convention in the hall of the House, and were joined by the Governor and Council. Col. Lane, of the Senate, chairman of the committee of reception, then came in with the President and his *suite*, and conducted the former to the area in front of the Speaker's chair. Hon. Moses Norris Jr, presiding officer of the convention, now addressed him as follows.

Mr. President. We are glad to see you, and especially to meet and receive you here in the hall of the State Capitol, amidst the representatives of our people. These crowded galleries and hall, the thronged streets and avenues of this usually quiet town, bespeak the ardent wishes of the people to see you, and to exchange congratulations, as American Citizens, with the Chief Executive Magistrate of our great and flourishing Union. This proclaims your welcome more forcibly than any words I can utter. Though in New England, and especially in New Hampshire, we have a climate of frosts and snows for a large part of the year, a country of rugged (though, at this season of the year, of beautiful and charming) aspect, yet we have a population, energetic, bold, and ready at all times to defend the country and its institutions, but of warm hearts and hospitable feelings.

We are glad to see you here, as the honored representative of the whole people, and of every section of our broad republic, that you may witness our prosperity in agriculture, in commerce, in manufactures, and observe our progress in the arts; and above all, that you may witness the industrial habits and general intelligence of our citizens, so essential to the prosperity and happiness of the people of our common country.

Sir, in behalf of the people of New Hampshire, and of the legislature here assembled, I bid you a welcome, a most hearty welcome, among them. In their behalf, I extend to you, not as the President of a party, but as the President of the whole people, their kindest hospitalities, so long as you remain amongst them.

The President responded with much earnestness and feeling. He said,

I am deeply sensible of the honor you have conferred on me by the cordial and distinguished welcome in the capital of New Hampshire. To the people of your State, to the members of your Legislature, and to you, Sir, as their organ, I tender all I have to give—my thanks. My visit to New Hampshire is full of interest, in the associations of the past, and in the present happy and prosperous condition of all I see around me. She is one of the old thirteen states that united their voices in that astounding declaration which first proclaimed the great principle that man is capable of governing himself. That august declaration, so emphatically announced by your ancestors and mine, was effectively sustained, and we witness now the extent of its progress and the grandeur of its results. After the lapse of more than half a century, one who was not then in being has been called to preside over the public concerns of the mighty confederacy, which, by that declaration, was awakened into life. This responsible position has been assigned under Providence to me; and in passing through the States I have recently had the honor to visit, in witnessing their vast interests, diversified pursuits and exhaustless resources, and in observing the diffused intelligence, robust industry and sound intelligence of their people, I have felt more than ever my great responsibilities to my country, and deeper has become my anxiety to study its welfare. But I rejoice to know that these responsibilities, weighty as they are, are not mine alone, but are shared with you, and with all my fellow citizens; for here, it is not with the rulers but with the people, that abide the strength and glory of our free institutions; the stability and permanence of our happy Union.

To this people is confided the last hope of man for well-regulated self government, and if our system fails, where shall we look hereafter, for another experiment which shall hold out a higher promise of success! With what veneration and gratitude, then, should we regard the memory of our fathers who founded institutions so full of promise, and with what ceaseless vigilance and care, should we watch for their preservation. In the achievements of the revolution, New Hampshire can justly boast of her Sages in Council, and of her gallant soldiers and no less gallant leaders in the field. Passing this morning by the grave of one of these heroic spirits of your state, who gave lustre, by his bravery, to the brilliant deeds of our nation's infant struggles, I was reminded that New Hampshire was still the same patriotic state that she was in 1776, for her young men and her gallant leaders are even now in the tented field, fighting the battles and maintaining the cause of her common country.

To sustain my country's interests and preserve her honor unimpaired, has been, also, my effort in the station I have been called to occupy, at a momentous period of public affairs. In this period, great questions have arisen and been decided, whose final results, must excite the most earnest interest of the whole union. Whatever they may be, I have the consciousness, to rest on, of having endeavored to faithfully discharge my duty, always humbly relying on the Providence of Him in whose hands are the destinies of men and of nations. I shall continue to do so, hoping, when I retire from the high trust which my fellow citizens have honored me, to leave to my successor the Union prosperous and happy as you have now described it to be, and as I have rejoiced to find it, through those parts of which I have lately traversed. Sir, my heart is full of gratitude for the generous reception I have met from your authorities and your people, since I entered within the boundaries of your State, and it will give me sincere pleasure, in accepting your invitation, to exchange salutations with your citizens, and so far as I may be able to do so, to take them by the hand. My visit, however, must necessarily be brief, in consequence of my early return to my official duties in Washington. I renew to you, sir, the expression of my thanks for your kindness, and beg you and those whom you represent, to believe, that I shall carry with me from New Hampshire, a deep and earnest sense of the cordial and distinguished welcome with which it has been pleased on this occasion to honor me.

After an introduction to the members of the Legislature and the Council, the President now withdrew, and returned, with his *suite*, to his lodgings. The Convention then rose, and both branches soon after adjourned.

At five o'clock we had dinner, Governor Williams presiding, and the long table in Gass's hall crowded with guests. The entertainment was a very handsome one, and was enjoyed in a spirit worthy of it. Unlike that at Boston or Lowell, it was enlivened by claret, madeira, sherry, and champagne.

At six o'clock the President was again conducted to the State House, where he was introduced to a great multitude of ladies. Mr Buchanan was of course not absent on this occasion, and among the ladies the bachelor premier was almost a match for the married President.

At half past eight P.M. accompanied by a portion of the Concord Committee, the Mayor of Lowell and Committee, and his own extended suite, the President left Concord by a special train for Lowell. At the depot was an immense crowd, full of enthusiasm, and we took our departure amid prolonged and deafening cheers. On our way down, we stopped at Manchester, a manufacturing place (where the people didn't know they had been ruined) and at the depot we found a great gathering of the operatives of the town, who thronged all points of observation, that, even by lamplight, they might catch a glimpse of the President. He stepped upon the platform and exchanged with them a passing salutation. The cars then dashed on, and in an instant the huzzas of thousands of voices and the spirit stirring music of the military band, were left far behind us.

At half past ten we took tea in the Merrimack House, Lowell, and at a late hour, we retired to our beds, with the full consciousness that we had passed a most agreeable day. The Granite Hills of New Hampshire contain a population of warm hearts and generous impulses. No where was the President treated with more unreserved kindness, and no where did the feelings of the people seem to go out to meet him, with such a spontaneous gush of enthusiastic regard. The authorities of Lowell, too, deserve our long remembrance, for their hospitable reception, and constant civilities while we remained their guests. The city of Spindles was found, by us at least, to be a city of courtesies and kindness. We found here A. Haines Esq. and S. Wells Esq. of Portland, Capt. J. C. Long, of Exeter, and various other gentlemen, who bore invitations to the President from their respective towns. A committee from Providence (R. I.) was very earnest that he would give that State a call on his return home.

Friday July 2

[Arrival Portland]

We took the seven o'clock train this morning for the Wilmington Junction, where we said farewell to our Lowell friends, and then started for Portland, Maine. At Haverhill, a thriving town on the Merrimack, we were welcomed by a salute of artillery, and there

was a large crowd of ladies & gentlemen at the depot waiting
to see the President. He gave them five minutes time, and was
introduced to them by Hon. George Lavary. Then we moved
on to Exeter, a factory town on a branch of the Piscataqua,
where a similar presentation took place, Capt. Long and Henry
T. French Esq. addressing the President, who made a brief and
appropriate reply. At New Market (N. H.) there was a fresh
crowd and a new introduction, and so there were at Dover. At
South Berwick (Maine) we received full deputations from the pine-
tree state. Wm P. Haines, of the Senate, and Hannibal Hamlin
and Thomas Chadwick, of the House, were a Committee of the
Legislature; John Anderson, Wm D. Little and Moody F. Walker,
of the City Council of Portland; Jos. Howard and C. L. Clepp an
additional committee of the people of Portland; and R. D. Rice,
G. W. Stanley and David Bronson, a committee from the Citizens
of the Kennebec. Colonels W. Cutter and G. F. Shepley, Aids
to the Governor, also joined us at this place. The address of
welcome was made by W. P. Haines, chairman of the Legislative
Committee, as follows.

Mr. President. We have repaired to this place to meet you by
direction of the legislature of Maine. We have come to bid you welcome
to our State. You come, the first of all the Presidents since she was
admitted into the Sisterhood of States. You come also for the first
time; and though you may have met with a more pompous reception
elsewhere, you have witnessed nowhere more sincere respect, and found
no warmer friendship, no truer hearts, than you will find among us. For,
be assured, far off as we are from the central seat of power, on the verge
of this confederacy, in the northern clime, we yet love our glorious Union
with a love, we trust, as warm and as true as that of our fathers who
formed it. And we love, also, the honored representative of the people
of this Union, the Chief Magistrate who, under God, holds in his hands
the destinies of this great republic. Nor can we, Sir, exhibit to you
those evidences of vast wealth which you have seen elsewhere; but we
can point you to native resources, and natural advantages for business
on the land and commerce on the ocean, unsurpassed anywhere. We
can point you to thriving villages and happy homes, to the school house
and the parish church, around which gather our holiest cares and our
warmest affections. Above all, Sir, we can point you to a hardy, honest,
industrious and intelligent yeomanry, of whom we may well say to the

distinguished chief of such people, as did the Roman matron of her sons, "These are our Jewels!" Amongst such a people, proud to receive you without distinction of party, and always rejoicing in an upright, energetic and beneficent administration of the general government, we again bid you a cordial welcome.

The President replied briefly.

He was not aware before, that no President had previously visited Maine since she became a State, but he was gratified that the opportunity of such a visit had been accorded to him. It would give him pleasure to accompany his Eastern friends to the flourishing capital of their State, and to observe on his way thither, those evidences of its resources and its prosperity, of which he had heard so much, and which he was prepared fully to appreciate. For the most generous welcome extended to him by the United Legislature of the State, he returned his warmest thanks, and he begged to assure the committees that, although his residence among their citizens would necessarily be short, yet he should bear with him to his home a deep remembrance of the cordial and most respectful manner, in which they had invited him to their borders, and bid him welcome to their hospitalities and their hearts.

After a short pause, and the usual introduction and cheers, at Saco, we arrived in Portland about half past eleven o'clock. Eliphalet Greely Esq, Mayor, addressed him in suitable terms of welcome, and the President briefly returned his thanks. Governor Dana was also in waiting at the depot, with many other distinguished citizens, and they were all introduced to the President, without delay. A fine procession was then formed, under the direction of General W. P. Smith, the President and his suite in barouches, Capt. Wilson & the Light Infantry in escort, and a noble body of firemen being among the associations which did honor to the occasion. The hill-side overlooking the *depot*, was crowded when the procession started, with a multitude of men, women and children, and presented a spectacle at once animated and interesting. Amid numerous cheers and surrounded by a living ocean of humanity, we moved up State Street, which was lined on either side with the pupils of the public schools, all dressed in uniform; and then we pursued our way through parts of Free, Congress and Cumberland streets, around the promenade on Mount Joy, up Fore and Middle Streets, to Mrs Jones's boarding house. Thence after a short interval, we went to the Exchange, where the President appeared on the balcony and was introduced to the people.

At about half past four, we had dinner at the U.S. Hotel, and we were called from the tables in order to be in season for the Augusta boat. The Steamer Huntress, Captain Kimball, had been employed for the occasion, and we embarked on board of her about six o'clock. There was a dense multitude at the wharf, and our departure was announced by tumultuous cheers. Portland is one of the most beautiful cities in the world. It is a peninsula at the head of Casco Bay. Its buildings run along on a narrow tongue of land, shaped somewhat like a saddle, Mount Joy at one end and Bramball's Hill at the other. Around each of these hills the citizens have made a broad promenade, and from that of Mt. Joy, the view is surprisingly fine. The streets are very neat in their appearance, and the number of elegant mansions is remarkable, for a place no larger. Its population is about twenty thousand. It was formerly called Falmouth, and was burnt by Mowatt, before the declaration of independence. During the last war the commanders of the Enterprise and Boxer were buried there. Its reception of the President did it credit. Mr Buchanan must have been delighted with its display of ladies, and the President was almost crushed by their generous bouquets.

Yet we had to leave them. We had a delightful trip down the bay and among the islands, and every thing was quiet up the Kennebeck, until we reached Bath, where a salute was fired, and the President was presented for a few moments to a large concourse of citizens on the wharf. Their cheers sounded their farewell, as we again pursued our way. Bath is a ship-owning place of considerable importance. At Richmond, a small town, farther on, our approach was announced by the ringing of bells, and the glare of bonfires, and the booming sound of cannon, and we were also saluted in passing Gardiner. We reached Hallowell at half past twelve, and took carriages for Augusta, where a most brilliant reception awaited us. The sound of cannon and of bells rent the air, rockets illuminated the sky, and for a mile in length, the houses and trees were beautifully illuminated. The State House, thus elegantly lighted, presented a splendid spectacle.

Under these auspices we entered Augusta, followed by thousands of citizens who added to the excitement of the scene, by their continued huzzas. The President had rooms at the mansion of Hon. Reuel Williams, and his friends were hospitably entertained at the dwellings of other gentlemen in the place. We found our pillows about two o'clock Saturday morning.

Saturday July 3

[Reception Augusta]

Early the next forenoon the President was met by his suite at Mr Williams's, and at eleven o'clock a procession was formed, under direction of Genl. A. Redington, on the Kennebec bridge, where the Presidential party was received by it. The Rifle Group, Capt. Timmons, did escort duty, and there were lodges of Odd Fellows in the procession in full regalia, while a cavalcade of citizens brought up the rear. The procession halted in front of the State House about twelve o'clock, and the President and his friends were conducted to the hall of the House of Representatives, where, as in Concord, all branches of the State Government were met together. Governor Dana, from the Speaker's Chair, welcomed the President to the Capital in the following address.

Mr. President. Permit me, as the organ of the Constituted authorities of Maine, to tender to you its courtesies and hospitalities. We tender them to you as the Chief Magistrate of a republic, whose youthful energy and progress give true evidence that in her approaching maturity she must exercise a controlling influence upon the destinies of the world. We tender them to you personally, as one honorably identified with and giving direction to events, which, in their momentous consequences, may mark the term of your administration, as one of the most important periods in our nation's history. We beg you, too, as the Representative of the whole Union, to regard your cordial welcome as an evidence, that Maine, in her sympathies, knows no geographical limits, as a pledge that she will never permit her patriotic attachment to every portion of the Confederacy to be weakened by appeals to Sectional prejudices and local jealousies. In judging of the capabilities of our State, we would with pride, direct your attention to our commercial, fishing, lumbering, mineral, agricultural and manufacturing resources, and ask you to count, if you can, their value and importance, or fix upon the date of their exhaustion.

Permit me, again, in behalf of our citizens, to bid you a most hearty and cordial welcome to our State.

The President stood in the area in front of the Clerk's Desk, as he replied, and his response, on this occasion, was more extended and elaborate than any other which he delivered on his Journey. The following is a full report of it.

Sir. It seldom happens that the course of any man's life is marked by so distinguished a reception as that which has been accorded to me today. I have been met, not only by the cordial hospitalities of your citizens, but have now received, through you their constituted organ, a welcome equally generous, from the highest authorities of your State. While with all my heart, I tender to you and to those whom you represent, my grateful thanks for the honor which has been thus conferred upon me, I feel that I can in no sense appropriate it to any considerations merely personal to myself. It is a homage paid to the institutions under which we live, and I receive it, therefore, only as the servant of the people, called upon by their suffrages to administer for a brief period, their own government. In such a capacity, more than in any other, I am proud and rejoiced to meet you on this interesting occasion, and to exchange with you and with my fellow-citizens here assembled, those hearty congratulations which it cannot fail to suggest, both upon the prosperity of our people, and the continued existence and success of our invaluable system of free government. In other countries, the monarch rules, and the people are required to obey; but in this country, thank God, there is no monarch but the people themselves, no allegiance but to the Constitution and laws which they approve, and no power which they do not give, and which they cannot take away. While, therefore, I occupy, by their choice the high office of Chief Magistrate of the Union, I feel that I occupy it only as their representative, selected to execute their will; and it is my great ambition so to discharge the elevated duties which they have confided to my care, as, at the close of my public career, to receive the rich reward of their cordial approbation.

This sentiment is in strict accordance with the whole theory of our free institutions. Upon the Sovereignty of the people, and the responsibility to them of their elected agents, was constructed by our fathers, the great fabric which they have transmitted to us, of a free and united confederacy of independent states. It is a legacy of freedom, which we hold in sacred trust, not only for ourselves and our descendants, but for the future welfare of all mankind. We cannot, therefore, too deeply appreciate its value, or too earnestly seek to preserve and to perpetuate it to the latest time. During my visit to this section of our common country, and my observation of its condition, its pursuits, its great and varied interests, and its enlarged prosperity, I have become more than ever impressed with this important truth, and more than ever sensible of the inestimable advantages of our confederate Union.

Under the broad shield of our Constitution, are embraced flourishing and equal States, of various climates, varied pursuits, differing habits and dissimilar institutions, and there is no greater triumph of human wisdom than that which successfully achieved one common government, for so many different interests, and so many distant states. It was the work of a convention over which presided the great and good Washington, and in which were collected as noble a body of patriotic men as the world probably has ever seen. A spirit of concession and compromise pervaded all their counsels, and we live now to witness and to enjoy the fruits of their wisdom and the results of their self-sacrificing toil. Fifty-eight years only have elapsed since our constitution was adopted, but within that period the population of our country has multiplied seven-fold, and our territory has been extended from your own borders here on the Atlantic, to the Gulf of Mexico and to the far Pacific. Thus rapidly has sprung up, under the benign influence of our constitution and laws, a mighty, a free and a happy people, still advancing in all the intelligence, the industry and the enterprise which can add wealth to a community or give glory to a nation.

To this Constitution, then, and to the Union of the States which it establishes, let us all look, as to the pole-star of our country's hopes, and the surest safeguard of human liberty throughout the world. He who would inflict a blow upon a frame of society thus glorious alike in its formation and its results, would hazard a calamity which no patriot and no lover of his race can contemplate without alarm. Let the Union be dissolved, and instead of the spectacle which we now present to the world, of a united confederacy of happy and prosperous states, we shall exhibit, as the mournful fruit of dissevered councils, an extended series of petty principalities, without harmony in either, and wasting their resources and their energies by warring among themselves. Dissolve the Union, and the last example of freedom to the oppressed will at once be destroyed, and the only hope of man for well-regulated self-government will be lost forever from the earth. In comparison with the vast importance, and the sacred duty of maintaining such a Union,

how poor and insignificant are all our little local jealousies and all our
divisions of individual opinion. In support of the Constitution, however
we may differ on other and minor subjects, all sects and all parties may
freely and cordially unite, and before the altar of the Union, bow down
in common worship, as citizens of one country and brethren of the same
great family.

I was glad, Sir, to hear you say, that, as a member of the Union,
the State of Maine knows no geographical limits, no peculiar interests,
no separation of climate or of soil; and I have been rejoiced to observe a
similar spirit of devotion to the Union, throughout my extended journey.
Among you who inhabit this region of our country, a devotion to the
Union may well be regarded as peculiarly strong, for looking from your
most northern borders to the far south and to the most distant west,
there is no place where you do not find "the bone of your bone and the
flesh of your flesh," where you do not see your own children successfully
exercising the industry and intelligence and enterprise which they have
inherited from New England, to work out their own happiness, and to
add to the common prosperity of their country. They carry with them,
as the children of other states bring here, affections and attachments,
which, rising superior to local views, contribute to strengthen in no
ordinary measure, the bonds of our invaluable Union.

You have reminded me that I am the first President of the United
States, who has visited your citizens since Maine became a State. I
rejoice that so great an honor has been permitted under Providence
to me, and that I thus have the opportunity to recommend here, as I
would recommend in all parts of our beloved country, the cultivation
of that feeling of brotherhood and mutual regard, between the North
and the South, the East and the West, without which we may not
anticipate the perpetuity of our free institutions. It was this feeling
which the venerated Washington sought to inspire, when he warned his
countrymen against yielding to sectional divisions or local jealousies, and
it was this sentiment which another Chief Magistrate proclaimed to the
world, when, in a crisis of peril and excitement, he made that memorable
declaration, "Our Federal Union—it must be preserved." What man can
adequately estimate the fatal consequences which must attend its fall? I
pray for the perpetuity of our institutions, not only because upon them
must rest our own hopes of freedom and of happiness, but because they
administer also to the welfare of mankind.

By the aid of steam, we are brought already into the close neighborhood of Europe, and foreign communities are beginning to feel the
influence of our system, and to receive from us liberal and enlightened

views. Animated by our example and the successful working of our
government, the suffering and the oppressed people of the old world
begin to understand now their own rights, and to claim the enjoyment,
as we enjoy them, of freedom of thought, freedom of speech and freedom
of conscience. This lesson has been recently forced upon them with
peculiar power; and the same ships which have borne to starving millions abroad the plenteous supplies of our abundant harvest, have carried
to them at the same time the glad tidings of our freedom, prosperity
and glory. They see us, as it were, the favored people of God, crowned
with plenty, and rejoicing in happiness, and their hearts yearn for the
same great blessings which, in our country, spring from the constitution, and are hallowed by the Union. Not only, too, do we thus benefit
the world by the great light of our examples, but we open here the
only free asylum for the oppressed which can be found on earth. Our
fathers, when they framed our government, invited them to our shores,
and we still welcome the honest and industrious emigrant, to participate
in our abundance, and to unite with us in increasing the prosperity of
our country. We say to him, "Come freely among us—act as an honest
man—and you shall be protected in all your rights."

The magnitude of our own national destiny, it is difficult even for the
imagination to appreciate. When this Union was formed, neither your
State nor mine had yet a separate existence. My destiny in my youth
was amidst the wilderness, out of which has since grown a state which
is now the home of a prosperous, enterprising and energetic population.
A similar success has attended the growing fortunes of Maine, and I am
rejoiced to witness your rapid growth in agriculture, in navigation, in
the fisheries, and in all the various interests which go to make up the
aggregate of your prosperity and your wealth. The same giant growth
is to be seen in all our territory, and is destined, if we are faithful to
our duty as citizens, to continue with increased rapidity through the
lapse of years. In this view, who can anticipate the future greatness
of our republic, and who can estimate its influence upon the affairs
and the destiny of mankind. If in fifty-eight years, so much has been
accomplished, for the grandeur of our nation, what results may she not
confidently hope to accomplish, in the half century yet to come?

When our Constitution was adopted, the individual who addresses
you was not in existence, and the man may be now unborn, who, fifty-
eight years hence, will fill the office which is now held by me. If the
population of our country shall continue to increase in the same ratio
as in the past corresponding period, he will then represent a people
numbering more than a hundred millions, while at the same time, you

in this eastern state, by the increased facilities of intercourse, will be brought into the neighborhood of our most distant possessions, and be able to communicate with them in less time, than at the period of the adoption of our Constitution, your predecessors could communicate with Boston. Let us hope, that at that distant period, when a future Chief Magistrate of the nation may be welcomed by a future Governor of Maine, they may be able to exchange congratulations, as we do now, upon the happiness of our people and the continued strength of our Union.

I have extended these remarks, because I feel that I can do no better service to my country, than to express, wherever I may find an appropriate opportunity to do so, my deep conviction that the preservation of the Union of these States, is paramount to every other political consideration, and that the same spirit of harmony and compromise in which it was formed, is vitally necessary to secure its existence and perpetuate its blessings. Throughout my journey, whose northern limit I have now reached, I have witnessed on every side, new proofs of its value, and fresh indications of the deep attachment to it which pervades the hearts of all our people. I shall return to my duties at the Seat of Government with an increased sense of their responsibility and importance, and with a confirmed regard for that venerated Constitution, which I have been sworn faithfully to administer.

Suffer me again to return my profound acknowledgements for the distinguished honor which has been conferred upon me by your authorities and your people. From this and a neighboring Sister State, I have received the most respectful consideration which it was in their power to bestow, a cordial and official welcome from their highest legislative and executive authorities. But let me repeat, also, that in acknowledging these marks of respect and kindness, I refer them all to the station which I hold, and not surely to any considerations merely personal to myself.

The President was then introduced to the members of the Council, Senate and House, and afterwards conducted to the rotunda where he was introduced to the ladies and citizens generally. At three o'clock we had dinner at the Augusta House, the Governor presiding, and here, as in Concord, there was no lack of the most generous wine. The only sentiment proposed was "the health of the President," which was received, at the close of the entertainment, with three most unanimous cheers. After dinner, the President said farewell to the people, and we then took carriages for Gardiner, where we were again to embark on board the Steamer for Portland.

We had an exciting ride to Gardiner. Every body who could get a vehicle followed us, and at every turn on the river we had a salute of cannon. Arrived opposite Senator Evans's house, the procession paused, and at Mr Evans's earnest solicitation, the President left his carriage, and was introduced to the Senator's family. We all had a glass of cold water here, and started again refreshed. This call at Mr Evans's was due to him, for the very liberal manner in which he had assisted in all the arrangements for the President's reception. We left Mr Evans's for the splendid mansion of Robert H. Gardiner Esq, whose residence is about a mile from the centre of the town. Here we partook of an elegant entertainment, at the conclusion of which, we drove out through the lawn of Mr Gardiner, to the village, and through the village to the steamboat landing, where a platform had been erected for receiving the President. We were conducted to the platform, and Mr Evans, in behalf of the citizens of Gardiner and of those of the opposite town of Pittston, then addressed the President in a very neat and well delivered address, which was received by the multitude around with repeated demonstrations of applause.

He spoke of the gratification with which his fellow townsmen, in common with all the people of that region of country, had received a visit from the President of the United States, of their distance from the centre of the Union, of their devotion to it, and their willingness to peril, if need be, everything in its defence. He then adverted to the resources of Maine, its extent of territory, its means of manufactures, its increasing commerce, its agricultural enterprise, and above all, its institutions of religion, of charity and of education. He regretted that the President could not see more of it—he would be hospitably welcomed in all parts of it—but he hoped that even the passing glance which he had been able to give to it, would impress him favorably, with its importance as a state and its general prosperity as a member of the Union. He then adverted to the congressional service which they had rendered together, and the uninterrupted harmony of their previous acquaintance, and concluded by wishing the President a safe and pleasant journey to his home.

The President was extremely animated in his reply, which was substantially as follows.

I feel, Sir, that I cannot adequately express my gratification at the distinguished welcome with which I have been honored in name, nor convey to you the pleasure which I have experienced, in witnessing the beneficent influences of our institutions, as they are every where displayed, in the prosperity and enterprise of the people of New England. I have come here, it is true, as the Chief Magistrate of the United States, but I may also claim to appear among you as a citizen, and as such, to meet you upon that common ground of equality which is the foundation of our republican system. In other countries, where the chief representative of the government is the ruler and not the servant of the people, if he ventures abroad amongst them, he must be protected by an escort of soldiers; but here, sir, the head of the government finds his only protection in the approbation and the hearts of the people.

You have been pleased, sir, to allude to the Union of the States as the occasion, chiefly, of our general happiness, and our unprecedented growth in all the elements of natural greatness. In this sentiment I concur with you, with the fullest assurances of my heart. We live in different latitudes—we are engaged in different pursuits—and it is natural that we should sometimes entertain different sentiments on questions of a local or sectional character; but still we are all brethren. Let us then adhere to the Union of the States, as our last hope for the preservation of those benign institutions, which, under the Providence of God, as his most favored people, it has been our great blessing to establish and enjoy.

The value of the confederate union is written in every page of our country's history, inscribed upon every monument of its success, and declared in all the thousand evidences which exist around us, of its enterprise, its intelligence and its rapid growth. Your state lies along the boundary of the north of a province under the government of a monarchy. Contrast the condition of the people there and here, and you will at once distinguish the manifest advantages which flow from the blessing of popular institutions. They are derived, all of them, under Providence, from the compact of the Union, framed by the wisdom of our ancestors, consecrated by their noble deeds and cemented by their blood. They have been felt in Maine, Sir, as fully as in any other state, for sharing the benefits of the Union, she has gone on 'prospering and to prosper,' until she has now become one of its most important and useful members. Yours, indeed, is a hard soil; but from the persevering spirits of its hardy sons, it has been made to smile with bountiful harvests. The energy of its people, too, has been equally displayed on the tented field, and even now her valiant sons are fighting, for the cause of freedom in their country, on the hills and plains of Mexico, and among them, I am proud to say, may be found your own blood.

Sir, I thank God for the unity of spirit which pervades the American people. If one point be assailed by a foreign foe, the spirit of resistance is awakened in the opposite extremity, and should the keys of Florida be approached by hostile feet, the hardy patriotism of Maine, side by side with the chivalry of the extreme South, would be ready to repel the intruder upon our common soil. Your commercial enterprise, also, is as unbounded as your patriotism. Wherever a sail whitens the waters of the ocean, there will always be found the hardy sailor from Maine; and wherever new houses, villages and town are springing up amidst the wilderness, there, too, in the distant west, as in the farthest north, will be found your energetic sons, felling away the forests, and opening the way for the onward march of civilization and christianity. Let us continue, then, to cherish our invaluable Union, and transmit it, as the choicest of earthly blessings, for the security and happiness of our posterity.

You have alluded, Sir, to our long personal acquaintance; and I am happy to remember, that, while we were together in the public councils before our heads were grey, and often differed upon political questions, we yet preserved always unimpaired the relation of personal friends. I reciprocate most cordially the expressions of good will with which you have been pleased to honor me, and return my hearty thanks to those whom you represent for the very kind and acceptable manner in which they have here received me.

Amid the cheers—long and loud—of the people around him, the President, then, was conducted on board the "Huntress," which lost no time in getting under way. We were off about half past seven. At Richmond and Bath, we had salutes again, and from both places there was a display of rockets. But we made no pause, except to land a few passengers at Bath, and arrived safely in Portland, about half past twelve. A committee was in waiting to receive us, and the President and suite were soon comfortably reposing in the elegant boardinghouse of Mrs Jones.

Sunday July 4

[Rest Portland]

Here, as in New York, the President avoided all appearance of public display on the Sabbath. He attended divine service (with Hon. John Anderson, Collector of the port) in the morning, at the Unitarian Church of Rev. Dr. Nichols, and in the afternoon he accompanied the Mayor to hear the Rev. Dr Carruthers, who preaches in the pulpit formerly occupied by Edward Payson. During the day he found time to visit for a few minutes Hon Asa Clapp, now eighty-five years of age, and an eminent merchant, as well as an old war-republican. He is the father-in-law of Hon Levi Woodbury. In the evening, the President met a few friends at the house of Mr Anderson. The quiet was no less beneficial today to his health, than in unison with his own feelings. One needs to have the six days of continued fatigue, in order fitly to appreciate the wisdom which made the Sabbath a day of rest.

Monday July 5

[Portsmouth Reception]

The President left Portland in a special train, at 1/4 past seven o'clock, for Portsmouth. A committee from that town accompanied him, and many good wishes and hearty cheers pursued him. The celebration of our National Independence occurring today, the *depots* all along the railroad were crowded with people who waited to see the President of their country. At Saco (Gov. Fairfield's home) there were near ten thousand persons, and the President was greeted in a very happy address, by Rev. Mr Hopkins, who is a whig politician and an orthodox clergyman. He replied in a strain of great earnestness and power. He alluded to the character of the day, the great anniversary of our national birth, to the happy condition in which it found us as a people, and to the lesson which it should teach us of attachment to the Union. He then spoke of the 4th of July 1776, when the American Congress was deliberating whether it should longer submit to the wrongs of Great Britain, or boldly and forever assert the nation's rights, and eulogized John Adams as the fearless patriot who, in that period of darkness and doubt, seemed like the Star of

Bethlehem, arising in the East, and pointing to Washington, as the Saviour of his Country. The republic which then sprung into life, it was for us to cherish, protect and defend. And he concluded by exhorting his countrymen to renew, on that day, so full of revolutionary memoirs, their vows of fidelity to freedom, and of unalterable attachment to our own invaluable institutions. At Saco, Benjamin Simpson, one of the Boston Tea Party, now ninety three years of age, was taken to the platform and introduced to the President, who received him with unaffected warmth.

At Kennebunk, Wells, North Berwick and South Berwick, there were other multitudes and introductions, as at Saco, and the President had to make several brief addresses, which he knew how to do. On the Piscataqua bridge, which connects Kittery (Me) with Portsmouth (N.H.) Hon. W. P. Haines, in behalf of the Legislature, and Col. Geo. F. Shepley, in behalf of Governor Dana, severally took leave of the President, and introduced him to Col. Ichabod Bartlett, Chairman of a sub-committee of the Citizens of Portsmouth.

The train reached Portsmouth about half past ten. The President and party were transferred to carriages, and a procession was at once formed, escorted by five military companies, and containing large delegations of Masons and Odd Fellows in appropriate regalia. It pursued its way, under arches of evergreen, amid immense throngs of people, and through extended lines of pupils of the schools, beautifully dressed in uniform, to a platform, which had been erected for the occasion in front of Congress Hall. Judge Woodbury here tendered him the hearty welcome of the city, in a speech which was both appropriate and well-given. He spoke of the fertility of the Granite State in producing hardy, honest and intelligent freemen, and of the neighborhood of Portsmouth as one of the earliest of the New Hampshire settlements. He alluded to their beautiful river, where their fathers came for a freer trade as well as a freer worship, and the navy yard near by, where was built the first ship of the line since the independence, and the first frigate in America. He concluded by assuring the President, that he had the best wishes of every heart before him for the happiness of his journey, and the safety of his return home.

The President, in reply, spoke of the importance of Portsmouth as a Naval Station, and said it gave him infinite satisfaction to witness the prosperity of the place and the happiness of its citizens. Having been introduced to the ladies of Portsmouth at Congress Hall, the President, then, accompanied by Mr Buchanan and many of his suite besides, rode over to Judge Woodbury's mansion, where his accomplished lady entertained them in a most elegant manner. The ceremonies were closed by a handsome dinner at the Rockingham House, at which Judge Woodbury presided, assisted by Colonel Bartlett.

The President arrived at Newburyport (Caleb Cushing's home) at a quarter past two. He was received on a platform by Nathaniel Horton, who made him a very short address of welcome, to which he replied with great success. The train departed amid a storm of cheers. At Ipswich, the President was induced to visit the residence of Capt. Lord, where in the presence of some three thousand people, he replied to an address from Josiah Caldwell Esq.

At Beverly (the former residence of Nathan Dane, author of the Ordnance of '87) the collection at the bridge (leading to Salem) was immense, but it having been arranged that the Mayor of Salem should address the President in behalf of both places, he was taken into a barouche, and escorted from Beverly to the Salem Depot, with Mr Buchanan and others of his suite. Here there was a great turnout of the people, and the display, both military and civic, was well worthy of the occasion. The pupils of the schools attracted peculiar attention, alike from their large number, and their handsome, uniform appearance. Had time enough been allowed in Salem, its reception would have been full of elegance and interest; but the President was compelled, in order to reach Fall River in time, to hurry through its streets, so rapidly that it was with much difficulty he could either see or be seen. The Mayor, however, Joseph S. Cabot, found time enough for his speech of welcome, to which the President very briefly replied. Salem is the oldest town within the chartered limits of the original colony of Massachusetts, and the second oldest town within the present boundaries of the commonwealth. It has always been a commercial place, and largely concerned in the East India trade. Wm Gray resided here, and it was the early residence of Judge Story. It was the birth place of Timothy Pickering, and Nathl. Bowditch, the mathematician. The witches were hung here in 1692. Roger Williams once preached here, and was driven away for thinking freely, and speaking as he thought. In 1774 Genl Gage ordered the General Court here, the port of Boston being closed. It is a city of great wealth, and contains about eighteen thousand inhabitants. It fitted out sixty armed vessels in the revolution, and Mr Cabot said that the first blood was shed, and the first successful resistance made, at the commencement of the revolution, in Salem.

At Lynn, a town of Shoemakers, there was another glorious reception, and the President, while standing in a barouche at the north depot, was addressed by J. C. Stickney Esq, but had hardly time to respond his thanks, before he was carried off at a rapid rate to the Southern depot.

He reached Boston with his party about five o'clock, found carriages in waiting at the depot, under direction of James Whiting Esq, and drove directly across the city, to the Providence R. R. Depot, where he took a special train of cars for Fall River.

At Taunton, Governor Morton's town, and a place of some nine thousand inhabitants, the President was received by a vast concourse of people, and addressed by Samuel L. Crocher Esq, Chairman of the Board of Selectmen, who bade him welcome to the soil of the "Old Colony." He replied with a eulogy of the Pilgrim character, and with his hearty thanks, and was then off for Fall River, where he arrived about eight o'clock.

Here there was another grand reception, and Hon Foster Hooper made the address of welcome. The President replied, bidding adieu to New England, acknowledging her importance, expressing gratitude for her kind attentions to him, and leaving with her his best wishes for her continued prosperity. He was then escorted down the wharf, and embarked on board the magnificent Steamer, the Bay State, for New York, where he arrived early the ensuing morning. He had celebrated the fourth of July in three states, and made some ten or twelve addresses.

Tuesday July 6

[Tour New Jersey]

After breakfast at the Astor House, the President, Mr Buchanan, Mr Clifford, Commodore Stewart & Captain Stein, were taken to Jersey Ferry, accompanied by Hon. Cornelius Lawrence, and other gentlemen on behalf of New York. Govr Mouton remained in New York; Mr Burke remained in Boston, and Mr Appleton had been left among his friends in Portland. On the Jersey side, the President and his friends took the cars for Philadelphia, and found himself at once surrounded by gentlemen from New Jersey, who belonged to various committees of welcome from different parts of the State. Among them were Genl. Wall, Govrs Dickerson and Vroom, Judge Green, Genl. Hamilton and John R. Thompson Esq.

At Jersey City, at Newark, at Elizabethtown, at New Brunswick, the President was introduced to the waiting multitudes from the platform of the cars, but at Princeton and Trenton (revolutionary places) the receptions were more extensive. At the former place Judge Green addressed him, and he replied with great ardor. At Trenton, there was a procession, around the city, by the battleground, and up to the State House, where he was welcomed by Judge Halsted, formerly in Congress, and one of the broadseal contestants. The President was ready and earnest in his reply, and concluded amid hearty cheers. He had dinner in Trenton, at Wychoff's, where the company had good wine and good sentiments. At six o'clock he started in a special train for Philadelphia, with a large attendance of Jerseymen, and at half past eight o'clock he was safely domiciled at Jones's. He supped with Mr Dallas, and had a good night's rest, after another day divided among three states.

Wednesday July 7

[Tour Concluded]

Mr Buchanan remained in Philadelphia, and Commodore Stewart did likewise. The President, with the remainder of his suite, left the Quaker City, at eight o'clock, by the regular train of cars, dined at the Exchange in Baltimore, and reached Washington at half past seven in the evening. He had been only three days, notwithstanding his numerous pauses, from Portland (Me) to the Capitol. He had been about from home sixteen days, and in that time had visited nine states, containing an aggregate of near seven millions of people, and had travelled a distance of fourteen hundred miles. He had more than complied with engagements made before he left home; yet in adding to his appointments, he did not forget to be scrupulously exact in fulfilling them. His health, owing to an exhausting illness which attacked him about the time he left Washington, and continued with him, to some extent, until he returned home, threatened occasionally to interrupt his plans; but he persevered to the end, and accomplished all his arrangements with the most perfect success.

No President could have ever had a more gratifying Journey. It was crowded with incidents, but not one of them unpleasant. The people bade him welcome, not only to their homes but to their hearts, and were glad to honor themselves, in doing honor to their President. The offerings of respect and kindness which he received were the more valuable, because they were purely voluntary; but they were also, on this very account, more elegant and more numerous. Such is the American character—millions for defence, not a cent for tribute—everything in courtesy, to a friend—nothing in extortion for an enemy.

The Journey was gratifying in every view of it. It indicated the vast resources, and magical growth of our republic. We enjoyed facilities for travel, which almost made distance vanish into nothing, and we saw exhibitions of wealth, of enterprise and of culture, which in so new a country seemed little short of marvellous.

We had an opportunity, too, to observe the deep love of our countrymen for their confederate union. Wherever we went, we found an attachment to our present government, overriding all regard for sections or for parties, and manifesting itself as a fixed, unalterable sentiment, too sacred even to be called in question.

Equally pleasing was the liberal and courteous spirit which was manifested towards the President by his political opponents. Party bitterness in America is sometimes said to be excessive, and the remark, unhappily, is not always without many proofs to justify it. Yet here was the head of a party, journeying through the land, as upon one continued triumph, and receiving, in many instances, the most hearty welcomes from those who were most earnest in opposing his election. The fiercest denouncers of the war paid him their highest official respects, and the most ultra abolitionists seemed to forget, for the occasion, that he was a slaveholder. True, he was received as President, and not as a party leader; but, then, there is clearly no danger to be feared from a political bitterness, which can be so easily restrained. The only exceptions to this universal appearance of respect to the President, were displayed by two isolated individuals, one in Lowell, the other in Concord. The former had a placard thrust from his shop-door, surrounded with black crape, and bearing an antislavery inscription; the other from an awning in front of his own premises, shouted, as our procession went by, "Hurrah, for the Slaveholder of Tennessee." These exceptions were so insignificant, that very few probably noticed them, and those who did observe them, only pitied the poor creatures who were mean and degraded enough thus to display their impotent folly. Had they excited general attention, they could doubtless have suffered summary punishment. They are alluded to here, because, considering the intense fanatacism which has pervaded many sections of the north on the subject of Slavery, it is highly creditable to the taste and general temper of our people, that the whole excitement was quelled, in the presence of the President, by the better and holier emotions of American patriotism.

The value of such a journey to the Chief Magistrate of the republic, cannot for a moment be doubted. He sees a section of the nation opposite to his own, and becomes acquainted with the interests, the resources and the importance, of distant communities as well as of neighboring states. He feels, also, (he cannot help feeling) a deeper sense of his responsible duties, and a more devoted love for a country, which he finds so full of all the great elements which constitute a people's glory. There is a reciprocal benefit, too, on the part of the citizens. As Judge Woodbury said, at Portsmouth, "We know and are known better, by being face to face and heart to heart; and it is alike pleasant and profitable thus to have an opportunity of drawing closer the cords which kindly bind together the true source of all political power, and those deemed worthy to administer it."

Of the personal bearing of the President, throughout his tour, and of the impression which he made among the people by his appearance, his addresses, and his general manner, this is not the place to write. It may, perhaps, be remarked, however, that, in the judgment of at least one of those who accompanied him, the occurrences of the entire journey indicated, not only a President contented with his country, but a country satisfied with its President.

The foregoing Journal, embracing, it is believed, the principal events of his northern tour, has been prepared at the request of the President, and with the hope that he may be able at some future day, to refer to it with interest and satisfaction. It exhibits, of necessity, a faithful sketch of a large portion of our country; and if another President should make a similar excursion a half century hence, it would be curious and not unprofitable, to compare the account of that excursion with the narrative recorded here.

It might have been enlarged almost indefinitely by adding to it the numerous incidents which related only to members of his *suite;* but these appeared rather to belong to the private memoranda of those gentlemen, than to this Journal, and were therefore studiously omitted. Enough is doubtless here, to weary the patience of any reader, in whose mind there are no pleasant memories of the trip to be awakened, but not too much, it is believed, to answer the purpose for which it is designed.

It has been written amid intervals of leisure, snatched from laborious occupation, and contains many imperfections; but it contains, it is hoped no essential errors of fact, and has been certainly prepared with an earnest desire to "nothing extenuate nor set down aught in malice." As it is, it is respectfuly submitted. "What is writ is writ—would it were worthier!"

Illustrations

View of the City of Baltimore. Engraving by Havell.

Adjusting Room of the United States Mint, Philadelphia. Wood engraving after Devereux in Gleason's Pictorial, 1852.

Merchant's Exchange, Philadelphia [1848]. Lithograph published by Goupit, after a drawing by Kollmer.

Girard College, Philadelphia. Lithograph published by Goupit, after Deroy.

View of New York from Brooklyn Heights. Lithograph published by Ives in 1849.

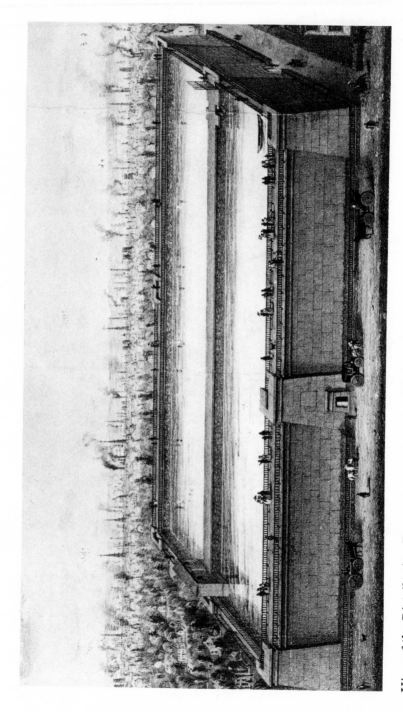

View of the Distributing Reservoir on Murray's Hill, New York. Lithograph published by Ives in 1842.

Astor-House New York. Engraving by Dirk.

The Custom House, Wall Street. Viewed from Broad Street. Lithograph published by Kerr in 1845.

View of the Boott Cotton Mills, at Lowell, Mass. Wood engraving in *Gleason's Pictorial,* 1852.

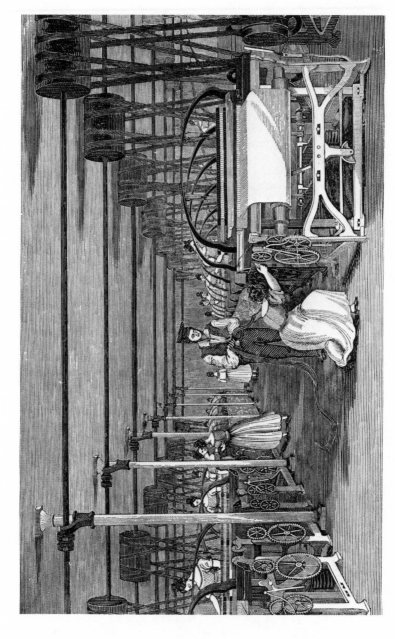

Power Loom Weaving. Woodcut in White's *Memoir of Samuel Slater*, 1836.

Portsmouth, N.H., from the Navy Yard, Kittery, Me. Lithograph by Parsons.

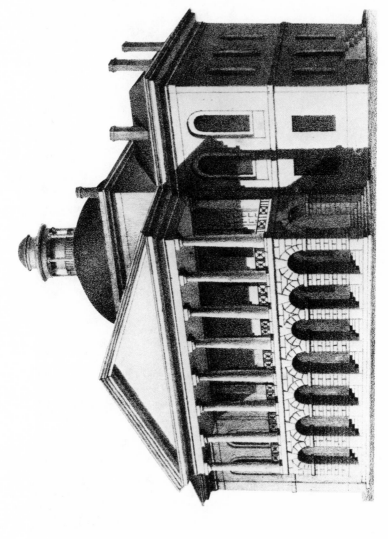

N.E. View of the State House, Augusta, Me. Lithograph by Moore, in Williamson's History of the State of Maine, 1839.

Tour Correspondence

Correspondence

From Henry Hubbard[1]

Sir   Boston May 17h 1847

I congratulate you and I congratulate those associated with you in the administration of our National Government on the brilliant successes which have attended our military operations in Mexico.[2] They can not fail to fill the heart of every American patriot with joy and gratitude. Having for a few days past been absent from Boston on a visit to my native village in New Hampshire, I was most happy to discover no diversity of sentiment or of feeling *among our people* in reference to the expediency of the war with Mexico or in reference to the manner of its prosecution and I can say with entire truth that all were prompt in their commendations of the Executive Branch of our government for their judgement, patriotism, energy and perseverance. During the last winter and since I have become a resident citizen in Boston. I had been accustomed to hear very different language from men in and out of office, from men whose hearts were callous to every patriotic feeling and whose lips were constantly giving utterance to their treasonable feelings. In my own state, from our hardy yeomanry nothing but the purest and most devoted patriotism was made manifest. No one could feel a deeper pride than I did at the declaration of such sentiments and such feelings from the people of my native commonwealth.

They are evidence of a proper spirit; they tell well for the country and give assurance that our free institutions are in no danger. They must be preserved and they will be preserved, notwithstanding the violence of Massachusetts treason. And now, My Dear Sir, will you permit me as an old and true friend to tender to you an invitation to visit New England in the course of the ensuing summer. Your friends would be most happy to see you and no one more than myself. Sure I am that you could not come

101

among us under more favourable circumstances. I should feel a great pleasure to meet you in this city and a still greater pleasure to attend you to New Hampshire, and there to introduce to your acquaintance as many sincere and unwavering personal and political friends as you will find in any other commonwealth, with no greater population.

HENRY HUBBARD

ALS. DLC–JKP. Addressed to Washington City.

1. Born in Charlestown, New Hampshire, in 1784 and graduated from Dartmouth College in 1803, Hubbard studied law in Portsmouth and entered practice there in 1806; he served several terms as a local selectman before winning election in 1812 to the state legislature. In 1829 he won the first of three terms in the U.S. House; he moved to the U.S. Senate for one term in 1835. Hubbard secured the governorship of New Hampshire in 1841, and in 1846 became U.S. subtreasurer for Boston, in which post he served for three years.

2. Reference is to victories at Monterey, Buena Vista, and Vera Cruz.

To George M. Dallas[1]

My Dear Sir: Washington City May 24th 1847

In answer to the inquiries contained in your letter of the 22nd Instant,[2] I can only say that I contemplate making a short visit to the North in June, but am unable to fix upon a precise day when I may be expected in Philadelphia, until after my return from North Carolina.[3] Much, indeed everything, will then depend upon the condition of public affairs, and my public duties in reference to them. You shall however be advised some days in advance of the trip when I will leave Washington. As to the "mode of reception," about which you wish to consult my wishes, I can make no suggestions. That I must leave entirely to my friends. Whatever "mode" they may adopt will be agreeable to me, only remarking, in reply to one of your inquiries, of a "public dinner," it strikes me would be unusual and not appropriate for one occupying my position. I could not I think with propriety accept a general invitation, to such a reception. I will cheerfully meet my fellow citizens, in other of the modes, which you suggest, or in such manner as may be most agreeable to them.

Mrs. Polk and myself, will take great pleasure in accepting the kind invitation of Mrs. Dallas and yourself to make your house our home, during our short stay in your city. The public reception, such as my friends may suggest, would of course be at some public place, after which I could retire to your house.

JAMES K. POLK

ALS. DLC–JKP. Addressed to Philadelphia.

1. A native of Philadelphia and a graduate of Princeton College, Dallas prepared for a legal career before serving in 1814 as secretary to Albert Gallatin, U.S. minister to Russia. Dallas returned to the United States and took a position in New York City as solicitor for the Bank of the United States. In 1817 he was appointed deputy attorney general of Philadelphia; in 1829 he was named mayor. Dallas was elected to fill a vacant seat in the U.S. Senate in 1831; upon completion of the term in 1833, he became attorney general of Pennsylvania and served until his appointment as U.S. minister to Russia in 1837. Elected vice president on Polk's ticket in 1844, Dallas served a single term and returned to Philadelphia. He was appointed U.S. minister to Great Britain in 1856 and held that post for five years.

2. Letter not found.

3. Polk planned to attend the June 3rd commencement exercises of the University of North Carolina at Chapel Hill, his alma mater; he left Washington City on May 28th and returned on June 5th.

From James Russell et al.

Sir   Boston June 2nd 1847

It is the earnest desire and hope of the Democracy of this Commonwealth that you will visit Massachusetts during the present summer. In this desire a very large portion of our fellow citizens of all parties fully participate.

We have been directed in behalf of the Democratic State Central Committee to convey to you the expression and assurance of this desire and to request you if practicable to include Massachusetts in your northern tour. We are fully satisfied that the moment it became known that the President intended to visit Massachusetts, the various state and municipal authorities would take that action upon the subject which the President's friends would personally expect and wish.

No duty could be more pleasant to us than the one referred to except that of giving you a hearty welcome to our midst.

And we therefore for ourselves and as the authorized representatives of our party most respectfully and cordially invite you to the Old Bay State.

                                                             JAMES RUSSELL

LS. DLC–JKP. Addressed to Washington City and signed by Russell and six other members of the Democratic State Central Committee of Massachusetts: Eliab Ward, John A. Bolles, F. A. Hildreth, Marcus Morton, Jr., W. J. Reynolds, and William E. Parmenter. Polk's nephew and private secretary, J. Knox Walker, responded on June 19, 1847, that the President anticipated visiting

Boston and Lowell on his forthcoming tour. ALS. DLC–JKP. Addressed to Boston.

From Isaac Toucey[1]

My dear Sir   Hartford Connecticut June 8th 1847
    The recent visit of the President to North Carolina has served to excite afresh the wish long entertained by the Republicans of the North, that he wd pay a visit, brief though it might be, to this part of the Union.
    There are many reasons why we wd especially press the invitation at the present time. In the midst of an administration conducted with the most brilliant success both at home & abroad, we shd like to point you to some practical results in this quarter. To say nothing of considerations of personal acquaintance & friendship, or political sympathy & attachment, we wish you to behold with your own eyes the ruin & desolation supposed to follow upon the patriotic vindication of national rights & the introduction of enlarged & liberal views into the domestic administration of this country.
    We can readily appreciate the difficulties attending your absence from the seat of government; but the facilities of rapid travelling are so great, & the necessity of a little unbending from the cares of State so indispensable, that we flatter ourselves you will accede to the unanimous wishes of your friends. Allow me to speak for myself individually as well as for others, & to promise you as warm a reception as was ever accorded to any Chief Magistrate.

                                                      ISAAC TOUCEY

    ALS. DLC–JKP. Addressed to Washington City.
    1. Trained in classical and legal studies, Toucey began professional practice in Hartford, Connecticut, in 1818 at the age of twenty-two. He won election as a Democrat to two terms in the U.S. House, 1835-39, but lost his bid for reelection. Defeated in his 1845 race for governor, the legislature chose him the following year to serve as governor for a part term. In 1848 he was named U.S. Attorney General, in which office he served for the remainder of Polk's presidency. He subsequently served in the U.S. Senate from 1852 to 1857.

From Anonymous

Sir,   Boston June 15 [1847][1]
    Your attention is respectfully requested to an article in the "Boston Daily & Commercial Advertiser," in which reference is made to your proposed visit to New-England: and particularly to Boston, should you

unfortunately intend to come hither. The nature of the reception you would meet, is in that article with great courtesy, but equal plainness set forth. And you will not fail in perusing it to be assured, that it expresses fully the sentiments of the most intelligent and influential citizens among us. The people of Boston can never be unmindful of the *exterior respect* due to any Chief Magistrate of the nation. But the reception of Mr. Tyler, here, sufficiently showed how well they can distinguish between a *demanded decorum* and an heartfelt respect.[2] You will not wisely consult the feelings of the people of Massachusetts or *your own*, in extending your progress to their borders, at the present time.

The unjust and atrocious war, in which you have plunged this country, and for which you are *personally* responsible before God and mankind; the presumptuous and mischievous exercise of pre-rogative, in regard most especially, to the Bill for National Improvements,† are too deeply considered and justly condemned, to permit the people of New-England to extend to you any other than the outward respect, demanded by your station. We have too much respect for ourselves to withhold *that*. We have too much reason to condemn your administration to offer you any more. Be assured, Sir, that you will be ill-advised, should you determine to make experiment of the people of Massachusetts.

† For this whole matter of your Veto be pleased to consult the American Review, or Whig Journal for June 1847 in an able article on *Western Improvements*.[3]

L. DLC–JKP. Addressed to Washington City and unsigned. Polk's AE on the cover reads as follows: "Anonymous. From *Boston:* Rc'd. June 18th, 1847. This letter advises me not to visit Boston, because as the writer states, I will not be respectfully Treated. This is no doubt the spleen of an old Federalist."
   1. Year identified through content analysis.
   2. Tyler visited Boston and its environs June 16–21, 1843.
   3. Reference is to the *American Whig Review*, a monthly publication issued from New York City, 1845–52; article not identified further.

From John K. Kane[1]

My dear Sir,   Phila. 15 June 1847
   Mr. Dallas tells me you may probably be with your Philadelphia friends on thursday of next week. We shall wait over thursday of this week to see whether the city councils will take charge of your reception,

or rather to leave with them the responsibility of omitting it, for they will of course extend to you the same niggard courtesies which they conceded to Gen. Jackson and Mr. Van Buren. But on friday we shall meet, and do all that a thorough-going set of friends can do to make your visit to Philadelphia agreeable. If you will let us know exactly at what time you are to leave Baltimore, we will have a deputation to meet you on the way, and if Mrs. Polk consents to accompany you, we will have things properly ordered, to welcome her.

J. K. KANE

ALS. DLC–JKP. Addressed to Washington City and marked "personal."
1. A prominent Democrat and member of the Philadelphia bar, Kane served as solicitor of Philadelphia, 1829-32; attorney-general of Pennsylvania, 1845-46; and U.S. judge for the eastern district of Pennsylvania, 1846-58.

To George M. Dallas

My Dear Sir: Washington City June 16th 1847
I promised you, in the event the state of the public business should be such as to permit me to make a short excursion to the North, during the present summer, to inform you, at what time I would be in Philadelphia.
It is my present intention to leave Washington on tuesday morning the 22nd Instant and to spend the afternoon of that day at Baltimore. On Wednesday the 23rd Instant, I expect to make Philadelphia.
Mrs. Polk regrets that her long deferred visit to her friends in Tennessee, will prevent her from accompanying me. She will set out for Tennessee on the same day on which I will leave for the North.[1]

JAMES K. POLK

ALS. DLC–JKP. Addressed to Philadelphia and marked "Private."
1. Sarah Childress Polk and party traveled with the President from Washington City to Baltimore on June 22nd; she departed Baltimore for Tennessee on the following day.

From Robert M. McLane[1]

My Dear Sir,   Balt. June 16th [1847][2]
The City Council will to day, upon their final adjournment, adopt a resolution requesting the Mayor[3] to receive you as the guest of the City, which duty the Mayor will I know perform with all the grace

and good feeling of a friend and gentleman. He will confer with Mr. Buchanan[4] to arrange certainly the time of your arrival. He agrees with me that the train of the middle of the day will be perhaps the most agreeable, though for himself he would find the early one entirely convenient. The Mayor will present you to his Fellow Citizens as the guest of the City, and I hope in the evening, you will find time to see some of your more particular friends.

R<small>OBT</small> M. M<small>C</small>L<small>ANE</small>

ALS. DLC–JKP. Addressed to Washington City and marked "private & confidential."

1. An 1837 graduate of the U.S. Military Academy and a veteran of the Seminole War, McLane resigned his army commission in 1843 and entered legal practice in Baltimore, Maryland. He won election in 1845 to the state legislature and in 1847 to the U.S. House, in which body he sat for two terms. In 1853 he was sent to China as special U.S. commissioner, and in 1859 he was appointed U.S. minister to Mexico. Following the Civil War he served two additional terms in Congress, 1879-83, and a part term as governor of Maryland, from which post he resigned in 1885 to become U.S. minister to France.

2. Year identified through content analysis.

3. Jacob G. Davies, Democratic mayor of Baltimore.

4. James Buchanan of Pennsylvania, Polk's secretary of state and subsequently the fifteenth president of the United States.

From Joel B. Sutherland

My dear Sir   Philada June 17th '47

I found this morning on visiting some of our friends that it was intended to bring your Excellency up *by the cars the whole way* from Baltimore & to meet you near broad st. To this I objected, and stated that Genl Jackson & President Tyler both came to Philada by water & that you ought to come the same way.[1] I then explained what was done in the case of President Tyler when he visited the north. I told them that we engaged a special train to leave Baltimore at 1/2 past 5 in the morning. By this arrangement the President had sufficient time to stop at the Democratic City of Wilmington in Delaware, & partake of any attention prepared for the occasion—that a Committee of 50 left Phila on the Ohio steamer the same morning specially chartered for the reception of the President and that by this route, he not only reach'd the city by 1/2 past 2 o'clock but he also had time to recruit & refresh himself on board of the steamboat & be prepared for the ride through the city & part of the County of Philada.

I added too, that by the river journey, you would arrive at the Navy yard & receive the same Presidential salute, that President Tyler did on his visit to Philada. Besides by passing up some distance *in front* of the city on the steamboat, the whole affair would pass off, with much more satisfaction to the people of Philada. I think it is probable that this course will be adopted & that your reception will be altogether worthy of the Chief Magistrate of the union. The Whig Councils will not make any arrangements for your reception by themselves *as a body;* but they will as in other cases, give you the *Hall of Independence* for the Reception of your visitors. A spot so sacred & venerable, from the early history of our Republic, that a partisan Corporation could add nothing to it by its presence.

My son writes the Editorials of the Democrat at Madison. In its columns to day I find the following.[2] It evinces that the Democrat makes appropriate selections. I have nothing from Wisconsin since my return.

J. B. Sutherland

ALS. DLC–JKP. Addressed to Washington.

1. Andrew Jackson visited Philadelphia and environs June 8-11, 1833; John Tyler went there June 9-10, 1843.

2. At this point Sutherland pasted a printed clipping on his page, the text of which reads as follows: "The Vera Cruz Eagle of the 5th inst., has a long article on the subject of Gen. Pillow's late appointment of Major General, and in opposition to the charges that have been so freely made regarding his competency. The editor of the Eagle, who was present at the bombardment of that city, and witnessed the important part which Gen. Pillow performed in that eventful drama, speaks not in the cuckoo notes of partisanship, but of that to which he was a witness. — *Delta*."

From Joel B. Sutherland

Friday night

My dear Sir   Philadelphia [June 18, 1847][1]

I have just left the meeting held at our Court House to make arrangements for your reception. John Swift Esq, Mayor of the city, presided. I lifted my hat to him, in the chair. When he said I suppose you are astonished to see me here. Not at all said I, as you are the Mayor of *the city* and therefore ought to preside. He made a neat speech on taking the chair. And the resolutions proposed for the occasion passed *unanimously* & so *declared* by his honor the Mayor. You are to *come by water* in the manner I proposed. The idea of bringing you through the dust from Wilmington in the car being abandoned. The meeting was large & enthusiastic. On my way home, I took a few minutes to write this at the House of our friend Jenks,[2] who came up with me from the meeting.

J B SUTHERLAND

ALS. DLC–JKP. Addressed to Washington City.
1. Date identified through content analysis.
2. An ardent Democrat and former party worker in Bucks County, Pennsylvania, Daniel T. Jenks moved to Philadelphia in 1845 and secured appointment as a clerk in the U.S. Customs House in 1847.

From Daniel T. Jenks

My Dear Sir   Philadelphia June 19th 1847
We had a large and enthusiastic meeting last evening to make preparations for your reception next Wednesday; the Mayor of the city presided.[1]
Those that had charge of the Custom House, were for having you received on broad street. Mr Sutherland & myself protested against it; had they adopted that plan you would of been covered with dust. I told Mr Forney to have you brought by Steam Boat; he said that they had agreed to do it from Wilmington. I am very anxious to have you received handsomely, and done every thing in my power to have it carried out. I wrote to one of the leading Democrats of New Jersey that you would pass through Trenton on Friday; they will have time to receive you there for a short time.

DANIEL T. JENKS

ALS. DLC–JKP. Cover sheet not found.
1. Reference is to John Swift, Whig mayor of Philadelphia.

From Louis McLane[1]

My dear Sir,   Baltimore June 19, 1847
I am happy to learn from my son[2] that you propose to be in our city on Tuesday, and that Mrs. Polk will accompany you. I am quite aware that the demands of your fellow citizens will fully engross your own time, and that I can have little opportunity of personally testifying my own feelings upon the occasion than as one of the multitude who will cheerfully unite in the honors so justly your due. To Mrs. Polk, however, it may not be so agreeable or imperative to mix with the attentions of

which you must be the object; and I write to assure you both of the great satisfaction it will afford Mrs. McLane and myself, and I may add my daughters,[3] if she will refresh herself at our house, and after dining with us join you at the hotel at your mutual convenience. I wish I could add the inducement which Mrs. McLane's personal attentions might offer, but the great calamity which her protracted indisposition has brought upon me still continues, and she is yet unable to leave her chamber, or even to walk across it.[4] In that chamber, however, she will be most happy to see Mrs. Polk; and all the rest of us will do our best to make Mrs. Polk as comfortable as possible.

If this or any other attention in my power be acceptable to you or Mrs. P., I would be glad to be informed of it; and have the honor to be ....

LOUIS McLANE

ALS. DLC–JKP. Addressed to Washington City. Polk's AE states that this letter was received on June 19, 1847.

1. A native of Delaware and a veteran of the War of 1812, McLane practiced law until his election in 1817 to the U.S. House, in which body he served four consecutive terms. He was elected to the U.S. Senate in 1827, appointed minister to Great Britain in 1829, named secretary of the Treasury in 1831, made secretary of state in 1833, and again sent to London in 1845. He headed the Baltimore & Ohio Railroad Company from 1837 to 1847 and resided in Baltimore during the ten years of his retirement.

2. Reference is to Robert M. McLane.

3. In 1847 Louis and his wife, Catherine Milligan McLane, had three unmarried daughters living at home, Juliette, Catherine, and Mary.

4. "Kitty" McLane suffered from a complaint diagnosed as "inflammatory rheumatism"; she died two years later.

From Robert Patterson[1]

My dear Sir   Phila 19th June 1847

The arrangements for your reception here will I trust be quite satisfactory. I suggested to Judge Pettit (who has taken the lead in managing the affair and is well qualified for the task by sterling good sense and firmness) that it would be a great relief to you, if you could come part of the way in a steam boat and obtain some refreshment and repose before you entered the City. In accordance with this suggestion, a special train for your use, will leave Baltimore at 6 or 7 o'clock in the morning—I have said this would not be too early for you—and bring you to Wilmington, where you will be met by the General Committee, and allowed an hour or so to rest, then embark on the fine steam Boat George Washington and proceed up the Delaware to the Navy Yard, where you will be received with a salute and other suitable honors and thence escorted by the volunteers to your lodgings. Judge Pettit, Wm J. Leiper & E. Jay Morris (the latter a whig) will go down on Tuesday Evening to Baltimore to see you, and inform you fully of the arrangements and see that all is properly conducted—both parties unite in receiving and doing you honor—please bear this in mind. I am anxious that your reception should be appropriate & agreeable, but I am still more anxious that you should make a good impression not only on our own party but also on the whig party. This I think highly important for future operations & results. To a man of your Excellent sense and tact I need make no suggestions. In my present position as a general in your army, I can not with propriety take a prominent station, or active part in the affair, but I will see that all is done right. In the mean time command me. You will find Judge Pettit a safe counsellor. Pray let yr position here be such as to give free access to all sections, creeds, factions, parties and fragments of parties. Let all have an open door and cordial welcome to the Chief Magistrate of the republic.

R. PATTERSON

ALS. DLC–JKP. Addressed to Washington City and marked "Private."

1. A veteran of the War of 1812 and a leading Democrat of Philadelphia, Patterson served as major general in the Pennsylvania militia from 1833 to 1867, during which period he held commands in the Mexican and Civil wars. His business interests included cotton manufacturing, banking, and shipping.

To Isaac Toucey

My Dear Sir: Washington City June 19th 1847

I received your friendly letter of the 8th Instant, some days ago, but have been so much occupied with my public duties, that I have been unable to give an earlier answer. You express for yourself and others of my friends, a strong desire that I will visit Hartford. I hope my Dear Sir, to have it in my power to spend a few hours at that City, on my contemplated tour to the North. According to arrangements which I understand have been made by my friends, I may be expected to arrive in New York on friday next the 25th Instant. On the monday morning following I will leave New York for Boston, via the *New Haven & Hartford* route. It is calculated that I will not reach Boston until tuesday. So that, if the hours of departure and arrival of the public conveyances in which I will travel will permit it, I will take pleasure in spending a few hours at New Haven and Hartford. I should be much pleased to have you join me at Hartford and accompany me on the short excursion to the North of that place and especially as far as Boston if you could continue with me beyond it.

JAMES K POLK

ALS. DLC–JKP. Addressed to Hartford, Connecticut.

To Levi Woodbury[1]

My Dear Sir: Washington City June 19th 1847
I have received your note of the 14th Instant,[2] enclosing one from *Mr Barstow* of Salem.[3] Should it be in my power, during the short excursion which I propose to make to the North, to visit Portsmouth, (which is at present uncertain) I shall certainly accept your kind invitation and am sure that I would feel quite at home at your house. Mrs. Polk will not accompany me to the North, but leaving Washington with me, will separate from me at Baltimore and proceed to the West to make a long deferred visit to her friends in Tennessee. She regrets that she cannot have the pleasure of visiting *Mrs. Woodbury and yourself* at your own house. *Mrs. Woodbury* has always been esteemed by her as among her best friends, and she would have taken sincere pleasure in making the visit, if she could have done so, consistently with her previous arrangements.

I will leave this City on tuesday next the 22nd Instant and according to my present arrangements expect to reach Boston on the tuesday following, the 29th Instant. I should be highly gratified to meet you at Boston, and have your company to *Concord* and such other points North of that place as I may have it in my power to visit. Can you not accompany me?

Will you do me the favour to address a note to *Mr Barstow* of Salem, informing him, that I fear it will not be in my power, during the very brief excursion which I propose to make, to accept his invitation to visit his home?

JAMES K. POLK

ALS. DLC–JKP. Addressed to Portsmouth, New Hampshire.
1. Woodbury was graduated from Dartmouth College in 1809, admitted to the New Hampshire bar in 1812, appointed to his state's Superior Court bench in 1816, elected governor in 1823 and 1824, named to the U.S. Senate in 1825, chosen secretary of the navy in 1831, moved to the post of Treasury secretary in 1834, returned to the U.S. Senate in 1841, and made associate justice of the

U.S. Supreme Court in 1845.

2. On June 14, 1847, Woodbury extended "Col. Polk & Lady" an invitation to visit Portsmouth. AN. DLC–JKP. Written at Boston and addressed to Washington City.

3. In his note of June 14, 1847, Benjamin Barstow of Salem, Massachusetts, offered to host a public reception at his home in honor of President and Mrs. Polk. AN. DLC–JKP. Addressed to Washington City.

To Louis McLane

My Dear Sir: Washington City [June 20, 1847][1]

I have received your kind letter of yesterday. Mrs. Polk is grieved to hear of the continued indisposition of Mrs. McLane, & during her short stay in Baltimore, will not fail to do herself the pleasure to call and see her. As she is to separate from me so soon, to make her long deferred visit to her friends in Tennessee, she thinks she should take rooms at the Hotel where I may stop. To you as an old friend I think I may with safety, venture to make a suggestion as to the hour of the day, I should arrive in Baltimore on tuesday next. I believe there are two trains of cars leaving Washington for Baltimore, the one at 6 A.M. and the other at 12 M. I would prefer the latter hour, if it should be agreeable to my friends in Baltimore. It would be a more convenient hour to leave than 6 A.M. and I think on other accounts is to be preferred. Will you make the suggestion to your son Robert, *confidentially*, and request him to write me, by which of the trains I will be expected.

It would give me sincere pleasure My Dear Sir, to have your company on my tour North. Can you not accompany me, at all events to Boston, if not further?

JAMES K. POLK

ALS. DLC–JKP. Addressed to Baltimore.

1. Although Polk clearly dated his letter "June 19th 1847," content analysis suggests that he wrote after June 19 and before June 21; note his reference to having received McLane's "letter of yesterday," Polk's endorsement on which indicates that it was received on June 19th.

From Louis McLane

My dear Sir,   Baltimore June 21, 1847

I beg leave to make you my thanks for your invitation to go north; and it would give me pride & pleasure to accompany you if it were in my power. The original doom of our race however, has fallen with full weight upon me. My destiny is to labor, and that in which I am now engaged is not a garden of roses. It so happens that we are fully occupied in determining our route to the Ohio, and the reports of the Engineers which are to have an important influence upon the decision may be daily expected. A temporary absence, even to Boston and back would be scarely excuseable on my part, so that I am compelled to forego an opportunity, which otherwise I would greatly embrace.

I presume you will have been made acquainted last night, with the Mayor's arrangements for your reception. He called upon me yesterday to state the embarrassment it would occasion him if you left Washington before 12 o'clock, it having been intimated that 10 might be a more convenient hour to you. The arrangements of the R.R. could have been adapted to either hour, but as I was sure your convenience would be promoted by not attempting to interfere with the order of the military I advised him to act upon his plans as previously formed. The superintendant has been instructed and has made his arrangements to assign to you and your suite, a new and official car[1] to leave W. at 12 o'clk and to place it in charge of particular officers to attend to your comforts and prevent intrusion. It will be entirely consistent with his arrangements that you should regulate the speed and stopping of the train to suit your own pleasure; and I have instructed him to conform in all respects to your wishes and orders.

I sincerely wish you an agreeable journey and a reception from your fellow citizens wherever you may go, suitable to a patriotic Chief Magistrate. Tendering my respectful regards to Mrs. Polk....

LOUIS MCLANE

ALS. DLC–JKP. Addressed to Washington City.

1. According to *Niles' National Register* of July 3, 1847, the new car was used first for the President's journey from Baltimore to Wilmington, Delaware. The *Register* described the vehicle as being "one of the most splendid cars that has yet been placed upon any railway in this country." Built at a cost of $2000, the car traveled forty miles an hour for part of the way to Wilmington.

From J. Knox Walker[1]

Thursday Evening
Washington June 24th, 1847

Dear Sir.

The mail of this evening brings nothing new or important. Nothing official as I learn either to the State or War Departments. There are rumors as you will see of the train up from Vera Cruz being attacked and some pack-mules being taken. It does not appear that much loss was sustained, but it is all vague & you will have as much means of understanding it as we have here.[2] Nothing of importance in any of your letters. Mr. Buchanan says he will not write unless he has a communication from Mexico, in which event he will inform you immediately & in the contingency mentioned of anything of importance coming, I shall not forget to telegraph you. All Well.

J. KNOX WALKER

ALS. DLC–JKP. Inside sheet without place of address; cover sheet blank. Polk's autograph endorsement reads, "Nothing new in Washington."

1. J. Knox Walker, Polk's nephew and a graduate of Yale College, served as the President's private secretary. During the President's absence from Washington City, Walker wrote daily to keep him current on reports from Mexico. Walker had travelled to the northeast earlier in June to make arrangements for the President's trip; unfortunately none of his letters, if any, relating to those preparations has been found.

2. The train of 150 wagons and 500 pack mules carried ammunition, provisions, and $300,000 in specie; it left Vera Cruz on June 4th and came under attack at noon on June 6th near the village of Paso de Ovejas.

From Alfred E. Beach

Honored Sir: New York 26th June 1847

Understanding it your purpose to extend your present visit to Boston, I take great pleasure in enclosing invitations for yourself and friends, to a ceremony expected to occur during your stay in that city.[1]

Your attendance, though but for a short time, will add greatly to the enjoyment of those present, and ever be remembered with pleasure by the parties to the ceremony and their friends, who would remain under still greater obligations, could you enter farther into the festivities, by performing the nuptial ceremony.

I need not add that the honor conferred in the latter instance, would command the highest sentiments of respect and esteem from its recipients.

ALFRED E. BEACH

ALS. DLC–JKP. Addressed to New York City. Endorsement in unknown hand reads, "answd"; Polk's reply has not been found.

1. Writing from New York City under date of June 26, 1847, Moses Y.

Beach, editor of the *New York Sun,* invited Polk to attend the wedding of his third son, Alfred E. Beach, to Harriet Holbrook, daughter of John F. Holbrook of Boston. The wedding was appointed for the evening of June 30th at the Holbrook residence; Polk's declination has not been found. ALS. DLC–JKP. Inside and cover sheets without address. Moses Y. Beach had served the President earlier in the year as a secret agent in Mexico City, where he had urged members of the Mexican Congress to support an end to the war; Beach had offered his assistance to the peace faction in establishing a national bank, which he thought might prove useful in financing a post-war government and its political friends. When Mexican military authorities learned of his proposals, Beach fled the capital city in haste with his traveling companion and sometime reporter for the *Sun,* Jane Storms.

From "The Doctor"[1]

Astor House, N.Y.
Mr. President: June 26, '47
Gen Thomas J. Green, of the ill fated Mier Expedition, desires me to hand the enclosed letter to you.[2] He would be pleased if you could only call at his residence for a moment. His lady, (late widow of John Ellery, of R.I.) had made large preparations to receive Mrs Polk, expecting her to come. Gen Green is from Warrenton N.C., a relative of Col. Hawkins,[3] and a Democrat always. I like the man, and promised him a word to you which duty being accomplished, I leave, sir, the subject to your discretion. His letter will more fully explain his location near Boston, &c.

"THE DOCTOR"

[P.S.] A word to me tomorrow through either of your suite will be a sufficient reply.

ALS. DLC–JKP. Addressed "Present" at the Astor House.
1. Pseudonym used by George B. Wallis, Washington correspondent for the *New York Herald.*
2. See below, Green to Polk, June 26, 1847. Green, an 1823 graduate of West Point, served as a brigadier general in the Texas army and as a major general in the California militia; he held a command in the 1842 Texas raid on Mier and subsequently escaped imprisonment in Perote Castle; a life-long Democrat, he won election to the North Carolina, Florida, Texas, and California legislatures.
3. Wallis met John D. Hawkins on the President's trip to North Carolina the previous month; Hawkins served on the arrangements committee for Polk's travels through Granville and nearby counties en route to Raleigh and Chapel Hill.

From Thomas J. Green

Saturday 4 P.M.

My Dear Sir: [New York City] June 26th 1847

Mrs Green and myself had fondly expected to have welcomed both yourself and Mrs Polk & friends at our house near Boston, upon your northern tour, and made preparations accordingly. Mrs Polk's visit to her friends in Tennessee deprives us of much of that pleasure but we still trust that you will make it convenient to call and see us if only for an hour. You and myself are of the same state, educated at the same school, & in the same political principles, independent of all which you cannot have a more heart felt welcome to the abode of any man of any party. Our residence is in the city of Roxbury less than five miles from Boston & a delightful ride from that city. The great crowd occupying any remnants of your time today has prevented me from saying this and much more in person.

THOS. J. GREEN

ALS. DLC–JKP. Addressed to the Astor House and enclosed in "The Doctor" to Polk, June 26, 1847.

From Elijah F. Purdy[1]

Saturday Evening

Sir: [New York City] June 26th 1847

My friend Moses Y. Beach Esquire, of the "New York Sun," informs me that his son has sent a formal invitation to you,[2] to honor him and his intended wife with your attendance, at wedding, on Wednesday Evening, June the 30th. The ceremony is to take place at the residence of John F. Holbrook Esquire, No 17. Ashburton Place, in the City of Boston.

It is near the Tremont House, and the parties are among the most respected Citizens, both of Boston & New York. It may seem strange to you that I make free to offer suggestions to the President relative to a matter entirely of a private character. I'll explain. Mr Beach is personally your warm and ardent friend. His paper whose circulation exceeds that of any other paper in this Country, has and is sustaining with *zeal & fidelity* your administration. Prompted to do this, no doubt, from principle, and a patriotic desire to advance the true interests of the whole country, and to mete out evenhanded justice to your administration.

Hence I feel, as an humble friend, a strong desire that, if compatible with your numerous engagements, you will gratify Mr Beach by attending, if only for a moment. Mr B. would feel the honor and duly appreciate it. He never forgets friends or attentions shewn.

ELIJAH F. PURDY

ALS. DLC–JKP. Inside and cover sheets without place of address.

1. Long active in New York City politics, Purdy served as an alderman and as a member of the board of supervisors. A businessman and banker, he identified with the Barnburner faction of the New York Democracy. He headed the Tammany Society and the General Committee of Tammany Hall. In 1845 Polk appointed him surveyor and inspector of revenue for the port of New York.

2. See above, Alfred E. Beach to Polk, June 26, 1847.

From Edward Everett[1]

Sir,   University at Cambridge 28 June 1847

Should it be in your power, while in this neighborhood, to visit Cambridge, I shall be most happy, in common with my associates of the Faculty, to have the opportunity of paying our respects to you, to exhibit to you the public establishments of the University, & to tender to you & to the gentlemen of your suite such humble hospitality at my house, as the hour of your visit may admit.

EDWARD EVERETT

P.S. The favor of an answer by the bearer is respectfully requested.[2]

ALS. DLC–JKP. Inside and cover sheets without place of address.

1. Everett was graduated from Harvard College in 1811, installed as pastor of Boston's Brattle Street Unitarian Church in 1814, appointed professor of Greek literature at Harvard in 1815, elected as an "Independent" to Congress in 1825, chosen governor of Massachusetts in 1836, named minister to Great Britain in 1841, made president of Harvard in 1846, appointed secretary of state in 1852, and sent to the U.S. Senate in 1853.

2. Polk did not include a visit to Harvard University on his tour.

From B. F. Hallett et al.

Sir,   Boston June 28, 1847

The Democratic Committee of the County of Suffolk, for themselves and as the organ of the democratic citizens of Boston, desire informally, to tender their respects to *James K. Polk* as well as to the President of the United States, on the occasion of his visit to Massachusetts, and to congratulate him upon the unprecedented prosperity which the whole country now enjoys, as the result of the democratic measures he was selected by the people to consummate, and in the fulfilment of which he has been as true to his pledges as firm and judicious in his means.

Aware that you visit this section of the union as the President of the United States, desiring no distinction of party in the reception tendered to you as such, your democratic fellow citizens have refrained from any public movement that should recognize a difference of opinion as to the measures and the merits of your Administration.

For every external demonstration of courtesy and respect becoming the occasion, they have relied (and as the manner of your reception has shown, with propriety) upon the known hospitality of Boston, and the just appreciation, by all her citizens, of what is due to the Chief Executive of the Union.

But while these demonstrations, which it becomes the constituted authorities to tender to the President, are publickly passing, in all the appropriate forms of official courtesy, the democrats of Boston, as the ardent and uniform supporters of the prominent measures of your administration, in a community where they are least appreciated and most opposed, feel assured that it will not be unbecoming in them, and they trust not unwelcome to you, to avail themselves of the medium of their Committee to convey to you something more than a mere formal expression of deference to the office to which you have been elected, and to add to it esteem for the man in his exemplary private worth, thanks for his enlightened public services and confidence in his fidelity to principle and his untiring devotion to the public good.

And in view of the extreme opposition the measures of your Administration have encountered in this quarter, we cannot but rejoice, that you will now have the opportunity of seeing for yourself, in the midst of the manufacturing capital & wealth of New England, not only her enterprize, skill and industry by whose touch the coarsest materials are turned to gold, but that you will be an eye witness of all this prosperity under the full operation of the revenue Tariff, & the warehousing system; the independant Treasury and even the Mexican war, from all and each of which your opponents who now reap the richest benefits, predicted the most unmitigated ruin to the country, but which are to distinguish your Administration as the era of free trade and enlightened finance, and the revival of national glory.

You will find here, Sir, in the wealthiest City of the Union (in proportion to population), and in the manufacturing cities tributary to it, the soundest currency, the safest credit, the free-est trade, the most productive industry, the largest returns of capital and the widest spread commerce that have marked New England enterprize and prosperity, as a whole, in any period of her history. And all this, the fruits of those very measures which have been more vehemently denounced here than in any other section of the Union, but which have proved so clearly judicious, safe and beneficial, that aside from the mere party politicians, few intelligent business men can be found openly to condemn them, while many who at first opposed now approve them; nor would they scarcely risk a change back to the exploded system, even were it within their power.

For now, in the self regulated currency and exchanges of the country they find a check to excessive importations from abroad, and ruinous competition at home, & surer than all the restrictions of a prohibitory Tariff, and safe and more wholesome, as a restraint upon rash speculation than all the cumbrous machinery of a National Bank, they once clamored for as the only regulator of trade, but which, had it been in operation, in the present condition of affairs in Europe, would have converted the surplus plenty of the land into general bankruptcy.

At the same time, under the operation of the reciprocal free Tariffs of this country and of Europe, the markets opened by it to the exhaust-less produce of the new States, not only enrich that section heretofore neglected in the national legislation, but immeasurably increase the demand of the West for the manufactures of the East, and the ability of our customers to pay as well as to consume. And even if there should be found some decrease of profits in a class of our cotton manufactories, the result is not attributable to the Tariff of '46, but to the enhanced price of the great staple of the South from which that section of the country draws a part of the profits heretofore absorbed by the North. In fine, Sir, in the results all round you, as you pass through our cities, towns & villages, you will discover, at every step, the practical demonstration of the fulfilment of the pledge you gave the country, before your election, that you would give your support to a Tariff for revenue, sufficient for the ordinary expenditures of the Government, and at the same time affording incidental protection alike to agriculture, commerce, manufactures and the mechanic arts.

With these expressions of our cordial aprobation of your public course, and our respect for the firmness, dignity, and devotion with which you have maintained the honor of the country, and added new lustre to her glory abroad, as well as new guarantees for her prosperity and enduring *Union* at home; we tender to you our personal congratulations & esteem, and bid you God-speed in the good work of establishing democratic doctrines as the lasting measures, and the fundamental principles of the free Institutions over which you preside.

B. F. HALLETT

[Endorsement] At a meeting of the Democratic County Committee for the County of Suffolk, held at the Democratic Reading Room on the 28th of June 1847, it was unanimously voted that the Address herewith submitted, be presented to the President of the U. States, and that the Chairman be requested to procure an interview for the Committee with the President, for that purpose, at such time as may meet his convenience. —Charles Mays, Sec'ty.

ALS. DLC–JKP. Addressed to Boston and signed by Hallett as "Chairman of Suffolk County Com."

From Francis Jackson

Sir,   Boston June 29, 1847
The Board of Managers of the Massachusetts Anti-Slavery Society request an audience at such time during your visit as shall suit your convenience, for the purpose of presenting an address on the subject of slaveholding, a copy of which is enclosed.[1]

FRANCIS JACKSON

ALS. DLC–JKP. Addressed to Boston.
1. See below, Jackson et al. to Polk, June 29, 1847.

From Francis Jackson et al.

Sir,   [Boston] June 29, 1847
Your visit to Boston presents a suitable opportunity to ask of you the immediate performance of an act, which is demanded alike by inflexible justice, the natural instinct, of the human soul, and the unchangeable law of GOD.

We address you simply as the friends of liberty and equality, in no partisan state of mind, and for no political object, with all the respect that may be considered due to your elevated station, yet with that frankness of manner and plainness of speech which an occasion like this demands.

You are a slaveholder. Men, women and children are by you held in slavery, recorded in your ledger as chattels personal, worked like brutes, without wages or stipulation, under the lash of a driver, and fraudulently and tyrannically deprived of all their just earnings.

No greater sin can be committed against GOD, no more atrocious crime against man, than this. He who commits it in this age of the world, and especially in a land so full of light and knowledge as our own, is pre-eminently guilty. It is man-stealing, an act, in comparison with which, the crime of theft, burglary or arson "whitens into virtue."

It is fair to measure you by your own standard. You claim to be a genuine democrat, and have been placed in the Presidential chair by a party claiming to be purely democratic. Is not this the fundamental doctrine of democracy, that "all men are created equal, that they are endowed by their Creator with certain inalienable rights, and that among these are life, liberty, and the pursuit of happiness"? Yet you hold men as your property, "to all intents, purposes and constructions whatsover," and do not blush! You kidnap human beings, and, like Pharaoh of old, refuse to liberate your miserable victims! With you, practically, democracy is synonymous with man-stealing; for no man would be regarded by you, or by the party to which you belong, as a true democrat, who should venture to denounce slaveholding as a crime. This is the extreme of human inconsistency—the acme of human criminality.

But, more than this, you profess to be a follower of Christ, and are, we understand, connected with a professedly Christian church, as a member of his spiritual body. How, then, dare you to make merchandise of those, for whom Christ suffered and died, that they might be redeemed in common with the rest of mankind? Did not he come expressly to set the captive free, and to put an end to all oppression? Has he not taught us to do unto others whatsoever we would that they should do unto us? What greater outrage can be perpetrated upon Christianity, than to make the profession of it compatible with holding our fellow-creatures in hopeless bondage?

The Bey of Tunis is no Christian; yet, "for the glory of GOD, and to distinguish man from the brute creation," he has nobly emancipated all his slaves; and made slavery unlawful throughout his dominions. Henceforth, every slave fleeing from any part of the world to Tunis is declared to be free, as soon as he touches the soil.

The autocrat of all the Russias is no democrat; yet, with many of his nobles, he has emancipated a numerous serf-population, and designs to extirpate serfdom in every part of his immense empire.

You claim to be a democrat and a Christian; yet you are a slaveholder, to this hour, an incorrigible slaveholder! Before the whole world, the Bey of Tunis and the Russian Autocrat put you to open shame.

The fact that you occupy a high station is no proof of your worthiness, but only demonstrates the gross wickedness which prevails in the land. Truly it may be affirmed at this day, as of old, "The rulers of the people cause them to err, and they that are led of them are destroyed."

Emancipate your slaves. Every one of them is your equal by birth, and an eternal destiny. The act may be attended with difficulties; but, be assured, it will redound to your imperishable renown, and in life and in death be to you a source of exhaustless felicity. But, while you hold them in bondage, your hands will be stained with blood, and your garments with pollution; and their cries against you will continue to enter the ear of the Lord of Sabaoth, until his judgments shall be fully executed upon you.

As President of the United States, if an American citizen should be caught in the act of reducing a native-born African to slavery, whether by purchase or violence, on the coast of Africa, you would officially pronounce him to be a pirate, and order him to be hanged, under the law of Congress. With what epithet, then, should you be characterised and what should be the punishment on the score of impartial justice, meted out to you, who are keeping in bondage scores of native-born *Americans?*

Reflect! GOD is no respecter of persons, and He is just! Hear, and obey His voice: "Undo the heavy burdens, break every yoke, and let the oppressed go free."

FRANCIS JACKSON

LS. DLC–JKP. Enclosed in Jackson to Polk, June 29, 1847, and signed by Jackson, *president*, for fifteen other named members of the Board: Edmund Quincy and Robert F. Wallcutt, *secretaries*, William Lloyd Garrison, Wendell Phillips, Maria W. Chapman, John Rogers, Cornelius Bramhall, Henry J. Bowdisch, Anne W. Weston, Eliza Lee Follen, Charles L. Remond, John M. Spear, Charles K. Whipple and James R. Lowell, *counsellors*, and Samuel May, Jr., *general agent*.

To Sarah C. Polk

My Dear Wife: Boston June 30th 1847

The reception at Boston on yesterday was highly respectful and gratifying. The day was hot and uncomfortable, but still the procession was large. Of all this as well as of the reception on the day before, at *New Haven & Hartford*, you will see an account in the newspapers. I am becoming much fatigued, but think I will continue my tour to Augusta in Maine, where I expect to be on saturday the 3rd of July, & from that point will return direct to Washington. I received your letter last evening written at *Wheeling*, and was glad to learn that your journey had been pleasant and agreeable.[1]

Almost all my leading political friends of New England seem to have congregated here, and will accompany me to *Lowell* to day. Among others *Gen. Woodbury, Gov. Hubbard, Gov. Anderson, Gov. Fairfield, Gov. Toucey, Senator Atherton* & many members of Congress, with whom I served in former years. In a word all my political friends are warm & enthusiastic, while, in justice to my political opponents I must say they have extended to me every mark of respect & attention, which my most ardent political friends could have desired. Thus far I am much gratified with my visit.

I received the enclosed *Telegraphic* despatch last night.[2] I have no doubt it is true. He informed me that he would take his wife with him to Tennessee, and will probably return with you.[3] I have no time to write more.

JAMES K. POLK

ALS. DLC–JKP. Addressed to Nashville.
1. Letter not found.
2. Telegram not found.
3. Reference is to the marriage of Polk's younger brother, William, to Mary L. Corse, daughter of the late Israel Corse; the young couple exchanged vows in New York City on the afternoon of June 29th, just two days following Polk's departure from that City.

To Sarah C. Polk

My Dear Wife: Lowell Mass July 2nd 1847
I have only time before the cars leave for Portland, to say that I am well & that I had a most gratifying and brilliant reception at Concord on yesterday. I expect to [be] at Washington on the 7th Instant.

JAMES K. POLK

ALS. DLC–JKP. Addressed to Murfreesboro, Tennessee.

To Sarah C. Polk

Sunday

My Dear Wife: Portland Maine July 4th 1847
After I wrote to you at Lowell on the morning of the 2nd Inst, I proceeded to this place, where I was handsomely received, and proceeded the same evening to *Augusta* (the seat of Government of the State), and arriving about 1 o'clock on the 3rd found the Capital & the

whole City brilliantly illuminated. On the 3rd (yesterday), I had perhaps as gratifying a reception as I have received on my tour. I was received by both branches of the Legislature, in the Hall of the Ho. Repts. and was addressed by the Governor, to which I of course responded in one of my happiest efforts. Afterwards I was introduced to as many of the immense crowd and especially of the ladies as could have access to me.

Senator Evans met me at Augusta & behaved very handsomely. At 5 o'clock I visited his family, in the town in which he lives (5 miles from Augusta), and afterwards, on a platform, erected on the wharf, just before going on board the Steam Boat to return to this City, *Mr Evans* addressed me in the presence of some 2,000, male & female, in a very handsome manner and in a very kind spirit, to which of course I responded, and my friends say I made the best speech of the tour. I can give you no more details, but content myself by saying, that my whole visit has been of the most gratifying character. The reception given me by the Legislature & Executives of New Hampshire & Maine, in their official character as such, were highly honorable to me, and were all that my friends could have desired. Nothing of a party or of an unpleasant character has occurred any where.

I reached here about midnight, last night, & have spent a very quiet day, having been twice to church. *Mr Buchanan*, Mr Clifford, Judge Woodbury, Gov. Hubbard, Gov. Anderson, Governor Dana, and Gov. Fairfield of Maine, Gov. Mouton of Louisiana, Commander Stuart, besides many members of Congress, with whom I have served, have been with me for several days. In a word I am highly delighted with my visit. On tomorrow I proceed on my return, dining at *Portsmouth* (Judge Woodbury's residence), expect to reach Boston at 5 o'clock P.M. and proceed immediately to New York, where I will arrive the next morning, and expect to arrive at Washington on Wednesday morning. My health has been good, but my fatigue has been so great, that I have been at some times almost worn down, & learn some of the newspapers have represented me to be in bad health.

Mr Burke tells me he has written to you to day, & I send you several newspapers, which will furnish you with many incidents connected with my tour, which I have not time or opportunity to write.[1] I have received no letter from you, except the one you wrote at *Wheeling*.[2] I hope you reached the end of your journey safely, and I calculate that you are to night with your mother & sister at Murfreesborough.[3]

JAMES K. POLK

ALS. DLC–JKP. Addressed to Nashville.

1. Enclosures not found.
2. Letter not found.
3. Reference is to Elizabeth Whitsitt (Mrs. Joel) Childress and Susan Childress (Mrs. William R.) Rucker.

Index

This book was designed and composed by the Editor on a Victor 9000 microcomputer running under the Xenix operating system and with the Tyxset version of the TEX computer typesetting program: text lines set in Century Expanded with display lines in Torino roman; reproduction copy printed on a Mergenthaler Linotron 101.